THE

GUIDE TO
MONEY

Mirror Books is an imprint of Bookman Projects Limited.
Published by Bookman Projects Limited
The Mirror Building, 33 Holborn, London EC1P 1DQ
First published 1993
© Bookman Projects Limited
Design and production by Nick Kent Associates
Spirella House, Bridge Road, Letchworth, Herts SG6 4ET

ISBN 1-898718-05-9

Printed and bound in Great Britain by
BPCC Paperbacks Ltd
Member of BPCC Ltd

CONTENTS

The charts and graphics used in
The Mirror Guide to Money
were based on information available in
July–September 1993

INTRODUCTION

By JOHN HUSBAND
Daily Mirror Money Editor

HOW do you go about buying or selling your home? How do you survive in the credit jungle?

In the course of a year we cover all these topics and more in Mirror Money, the Daily Mirror's award-winning finance section.

But your letters and phone calls constantly remind me that we never quite seem to be writing about your particular problem just when it crops up.

Many of you I know cut out and keep my articles. But those scraps of paper always seem to disappear or go out with the rubbish just days before you need them.

Now at last we have the answer. The Mirror Guide To Money. Between the covers you'll find most of the answers to your money problems.

It can't give you all the answers. Interest rates and savings best buys are constantly changing. And we'll go on keeping you up to date in the Mirror each day and week.

But for the answers to all the fundamental questions, such as what sort of pension scheme do you need, and how to go about insuring your home, and coping with debt or mortgage problems, all you need now do is dip into the Mirror Guide To Money.

Helping me to put it all together are a tip top team of writers, including past and present contributors to Mirror Money.

They include John Edwards, Ken Clay, Neil Simpson, Shirley Davenport, David Spittles, Malcolm Withers, Andrew Keenan, Margaret Dibben and Helen Pridham.

CHAPTER 1

MANAGING YOUR MONEY

BEFORE you can start saving you need to start managing your money. You need to know how much is coming in, and how much you are spending. Only then can you decide how much to save or borrow.

The old dictum of "look after the pennies, and the pounds will look after themselves" remains more true than ever today. Careful budgeting is crucial to avoid getting into debt. It gives you a clear idea of whether you are overspending, or have money to spare that can be put aside for the future.

How do you prepare a Budget? The first step is to draw up a Budget plan such as the one illustrated. You can either use this and adapt it to your particular circumstances, or buy a simple budget planner from most stationers like WH Smith.

The objective is to make it easy to see your financial situation at a glance. A good way to begin is to work out the income you receive - from all sources.

If you are employed the starting point is your payslip. This should show exactly how much you are receiving each week or month. Remember that your wages are subject to all kinds of deductions reducing the amount you actually receive.

Income tax and National Insurance are the biggest. But you might also be paying pension contributions, medical insurance and union or club subscriptions and possibly contributing to a share savings scheme.

It is the net figure, after all these deductions from your wage packet, which represents your actual income. A wage of £15,000 a year gross (£1,250 a month) could well be a third less by the time all the deductions have been taken into account.

Some of the deductions, like pension contributions and share savings schemes, should benefit you in the future. But they should be listed separately when drawing up your budget of income and expenditure. If there are several wage-earners in your household, you either show their income separately or lump it together to produce a single figure.

To give the full picture, other forms of income should be included. Unemployment pay, Social Security allowances and child benefits, for example.

If you have any savings and pay income tax, the net figure is the one that counts. Five per cent gross interest on £5,000 in a building society equals £250 a year or nearly £21 a month. But with basic rate tax automatically deducted the net income actually received is only £187.50 a year or £15.60 a month. So your budget should show income of £15.60 a month not £21.

Finding out how much you spend is more difficult. Take a look at any bank statement and you will normally see that the number of payments far exceeds the number of receipts. Money tends to be received in larger lumps. While payments out are normally a lot of smaller sums.

Once you start looking, there seems to be an endless list of payments. But you can simplify by grouping various payments together under key headings. Domestic and household costs; personal savings and insurance; car and travelling expenses; leisure activities. Anything that doesn't fit into these categories can be grouped together under Miscellaneous expenditure.

One problem is that not all receipts and payments are made on a regular weekly or monthly basis. Some, like road tax, are only made once every six months or a year. Another problem is that the amount you spend on food or drink, for example, may vary considerably from week to week. Then there are occasional payments such as buying children's clothes or birthday presents.

One way round this is first of all to calculate your income and spending for the whole of the past year. Start with the known regular weekly or monthly receipts and payments. Multiply by 52 or 12. Then add on irregular receipts and payments made throughout the year. Add the whole lot up. You can then divide the yearly totals by 12 or 52 to get a monthly or weekly budget figure.

There's no point in "cheating" and underestimating what you spend. It's much better to overestimate and leave yourself a safety margin. For example, if you estimate your total monthly payments at £500, add £50 to allow for things you might have forgotten. Or to cover nasty unexpected shocks like burst pipes, car repairs or vet bills.

Also bear in mind that although inflation might be low at present, it is still there pushing up costs which might not be covered by an increase in wages. For example electricity and gas bills are due to rise sharply as a result of the Chancellor's decision in the March 93 Budget to extend Value Added Tax to heating costs.

If you have a bank or building society account providing regular statements these can be very useful in helping you to check your budget.

A bonus here is that careful examination of your bank statement can often save you money. A golden rule for anyone with a bank or building society account is to check the statements or pass book very carefully. It is surprising how many "mistakes" are made - usually in the bank's favour. Furthermore banks have a sneaky way of adding extra charges without telling you what they are.

Only if you ask will the bank provide an explanation and possibly be persuaded to cancel the extra charges if you dispute them. Check the payments in particular very carefully. They will give you a good idea of where your money is being spent.

Once you've drawn up your monthly budget of how much you spend, you can then compare it with the net income you receive. If the monthly payments exceed the receipts, you will have to make a decision. Is this only a temporary hiccup? Or are you sinking deeper and deeper into debt? The budget will show where best to cut costs, if possible. It will also help you to borrow money. You will get a much better reception from your bank manager if you can show why you need to borrow money and how you intend to repay any loan. Listing your pension contributions, and any savings and investments, will also help give an idea of your future prospects. If the bank knows you have a pension or insurance policy maturing soon, it may be much more willing to lend you money. Looking on the bright side, what happens if there is a regular surplus of income over expenditure? First look ahead to see if there are likely to be some big bills coming up. For example, one of your children getting married. Or a more than usually expensive holiday. Or the need to buy a new car.

You can then decide how much to put by for the future, and how much to put into savings to boost your immediate income. If possible everyone should have a rainy day cash reserve tucked away, which can be drawn on immediately without having to give notice. Ideally it should be at least three months, or better still six months, income. It can be either a bank or building society deposit account. This should be separate from a current account used to meet your day to day needs.

Where should you keep your money - a bank or a building society? Competition has hotted up considerably in recent years giving you a wider choice. It is well worth shopping around for the best deal. The number of banks may be limited. But there are a large number of building societies offering the same or better services. For private individuals it is often easier nowadays to open an account with a building society than a bank. There is less paperwork and a more relaxed attitude. Banks want references to say you are trustworthy even if you deposit hard cash.

Banks still have the edge in offering overdrafts - one of the cheapest forms of temporary loans. They are also probably more suitable if you want to write a lot of cheques and use various other banking services, like direct debits.

However an increasing number of building societies are prepared to give overdrafts and loans too. Many societies also have cheque book accounts, which will also handle direct debits and standing order payments.

Generally building societies give better returns on deposit accounts, where you simply leave your money to earn interest. Building society postal accounts are particularly competitive. The lower costs of operating a postal service mean that they pay higher interest rates. In many cases they offer instant access to your money. You may get higher rates if you are willing not to withdraw any money for an agreed period - say 90 days.

Some words of warning. Try to make sure that you tell your bank or building society first if you find yourself spending more than you have coming in. Banks and building societies like to know what is going on. So if you don't tell them about moving into an overdraft you pay a heavy price. Interest rates on unauthorised loans are set at very high levels. And you are charged for "bouncing" cheques.

Your monthly budget should help avoid going into overdraft unexpectedly. If you feel it is a possibility make sure your bank or building society is told so that you can agree terms first. They will be far more reasonable.

If you are saving large amounts you should also be aware that the maximum compensation paid if a bank or building society collapses is less than £20,000. It makes sense, therefore, not to put all your eggs in one basket. Spread your money around.

Finally beware of taking advice from banks or building societies. They are under tremendous pressure to earn extra profits by selling endowment, insurance or pension policies.

Unfortunately most banks and building societies are also what are known as "tied agents". This means they can only recommend the products offered by one company. You are, therefore, faced with both a "hard sell" and a limited choice. The friendly manager has nowadays become an eager salesman - his job may depend on earning certain levels of commission.

The best defence is to take advice from several different sources. It may take time, but it could save you a great deal of money. If you keep your budgeting up to date, you will have a clear picture of your financial health. As Mr Micawber put it in David Copperfield back in 1850:

"Annual income £20, annual expenditure £19 9s 6d; result happiness. Annual income £20, annual expenditure £20 nought and six pence; result misery."

BUDGET

OUTGOINGS

Mortgage _____

Rent _____

Insurance _____

- buildings _____

- contents _____

Council tax _____

Maintenance/repairs _____

DOMESTIC

Telephone _____

TV licence _____

TV rental _____

Water _____

Gas _____

Electricity _____

Oil _____

Other fuels _____

HOUSEKEEPING

Food _____

Drink _____

Tobacco _____

Furnishings/equipment _____

Pets _____

Garden maintenance _____

TRANSPORT

Car repayments _____

- insurance _____

- tax _____

- maintenance/repair _____

- fuel _____

- AA/RAC _____

Fares _____

LEISURE

Holidays _____

Entertainment _____

(cinema/eating out etc) _____

Club subscriptions _____

PERSONAL

Clothing _____

Newspapers/magazines _____

Presents _____

(Christmas/birthdays etc) _____

FINANCIAL

Insurance premiums _____

Loan repayments _____

Hire purchase _____

Credit card payments _____

Education costs _____

Tax liabilities _____

MISCELLANEOUS

Any other expenditures _____

TOTAL OUTGOINGS   £ _____

INCOME

Wages/salary _____

Income from investments _____

- interest on savings _____

- dividends _____

- other_____

TOTAL INCOME   £ _____

less

TOTAL OUTGOINGS   £ _____

FINAL FIGURE: £ _____

SAMPLE
BANK AND BUILDING SOCIETY CHARGES

	Abbey National Current	Barclays Interest Option	Co-op Ultra	First Direct Cheque	Girobank Keyway	Halifax Maxim	Lloyds Classic	Midland Orchard	Natwest Current Plus	TSB Interest Cheque
Overdraft fees	none	£50 free	£250 free for 3 days	£250 free if over:	£20 free if over:	£50 free if over:	£100 free if over:			
Authorised		£5pm	£10pm	£15 a yr	£11pm	£5 pm	£8 pm	£7 pm	£9 pm	£6 pm
Unauthorised		£15pm or £30 if over £200	£15pm	£25pm	£14.50pm	-	-	£17pm	extra £3.50 a day over £50	£12pm
Overdraft interest *										
Authorised	22.4	19.2	19.56	17.4	17.6	17.5	19.5	17.4	18.97	18.8
Unauthorised	34.4	29.8	32.92	31.8	29.8	28.9	26.8	31.8	33.8	29.8
Charges										
Stop cheque	none	£8	£8	£6	£10	£7.50	£8	£6	£7	none
Banker's draft	n/a	£10	£10	£6	£8	n/a	£12	£8	£10	£5
Duplicate statement	none	none, £5 if typed	£5	£5 a sheet	£3	£5 (free fm machine)	£6	£5 a sheet	£6 min	£5
Bounced cheque	£20	£25	£30	£25	£19	£15	£25	£25	£27.50	£15
Receiving bounced cheque	none	none	none	none	none	£4	£4	none	none	none
Overdraft letter	none	none	£20	none	£13	£10	£10	none	none	£15

* Equivalent Annual Rate / Annual Percentage Rate

(See note on Page 5)

19

CHAPTER 2

SAVING
SAFELY

SAFETY should be the first priority for part of whatever nest egg you manage to put together. An investment in a go-go fund such as an emerging markets unit trust may do very well over time, but all stock market investments, and particularly those in the newer economies, both rise and fall with little warning, so you risk losing as well as gaining. You do not want to be forced to sell when prices are at a low point just because you need the cash right then.

You never know when an emergency will knock your household budget for six and you will need to lay your hands on cash quickly.

So put the equivalent of at least three months pay packets into some investment which will not fall in value and will allow you to get at it whenever you wish.

Here we will look at safe places to put your rainy day reserve. And they DON'T include under the floorboards or in an old sock at the back of a bedroom drawer.

For the first precious part of your savings, go for

* Safety,
* Accessibility, and
* Profitability - in that order or priority. If something offers a rate of return which seems too good to be true, it probably will be.

The safest place of all is NATIONAL SAVINGS. The government guarantees it one hundred per cent.

BANKS and BUILDING SOCIETIES come next. You are unlikely to come to any harm trusting your cash to the big well-known ones, but just in case you are worried, there are protection schemes to safeguard deposits.

Deposits with banks licensed by the Bank of England are covered by the Deposit Protection Board, which is run by the Bank of England. It will pay out 75 per cent of deposits up to £20,000, which means it will pay a maximum of £15,000 in the unlikely event that the bank fails. Overseas banks are not covered by the scheme.

Building societies have a similar scheme, but that one gives you protection for 90 per cent of deposits up to a maximum deposit of £20,000. Some of the smaller societies did get into difficulties in the recession and house price slump, but when that happens one of the bigger societies usually takes it over, liabilities and all.

Saving is not an easy business. But if you are reading this, you must think you can put something aside - whether it is for that 'rainy day' or for the deposit on your first home or a washing machine or whatever.

Probably the best way to do this is to take a careful look at your weekly or monthly budget and make arrangements to put away regularly each month as much as you reasonably can. You will be surprised how the cash mounts up if you do this.

Nowadays, investors are spoilt for choice. The banks, building societies and the National Savings movement all offer a wide range of accounts. The big lump sums get the highest interest rates, but you also get a bit more if you are prepared to lock your money up for, say, five years.

National Savings gets favourable tax treatment. Some of its products are tax free, but even those where the interest is taxable pay out in full, leaving it for you to settle with the tax man.

With rival accounts offered by banks and so on, people whose income does not take them into a tax paying bracket can register on an Inland Revenue form and have their interest paid in full. Otherwise these organisations deduct tax from the interest payments, although non-taxpayers can still claim it back.

NATIONAL SAVINGS

You may be surprised to find that National Savings offers ten ways of investing money.

Ordinary Account

This is the simplest. You can open an account at your local post office for £10. Further deposits have to be for at least £10 a time and you get a bank book to see exactly how much you have.

Interest rates are low. The ordinary account paid 2.5 per cent in August 1993. You could get a higher rate, 3.75 per cent, if you kept your account open for a whole calendar year. The higher rate is paid for each complete calendar month that the account has over £500 in it.

You can withdraw up to £100 a time at post offices. You can get up to £250 at one selected post office if you have a Regular Customer Account. You qualify for this if you have used an ordinary account at that office for at least six months.

Tax: the first £70 of interest earned each year is free of tax (£140 if it is a joint account) but over that you have to pay income tax.

Investment Account

This gives a higher rate of interest, it was 6.25 per cent in August 1993. But it takes a month to get your money out. You can open this account at any post office, but each deposit has to be for £20 or more. Maximum holding, £100,000.

Interest is credited daily. Rates can change at any time and will be available in the post office.

Withdrawals take a month from the time you post off a withdrawal form, which you get at the post office.

Tax: interest is taxable, but tax is not deducted at source, so non tax payers do not have to bother with forms.

Yearly Plan

The Yearly Plan is a good way of making regular savings. You decide how much you can invest each month, from £20 to £400, and arrange for it to be paid by your bank or building society if it handles standing orders. You get a Yearly Plan Certificate at the end of the year and can cash in or leave the money to earn a higher rate of interest for up to four years. Interest is fixed at the rate when you start the plan. In August 1993 first year interest was four per cent, with six per cent paid in the next four years.

Withdrawals: cashing in takes about two weeks. You get no interest if you withdraw before completing a year's saving.

Tax: you don't have to pay any.

Savings Certificates

You can hold up to £10,000 of the 40th issue, the one on offer at the time of writing. Minimum investment each time you buy is £100, which gives you four units of £25. Purchases over £100 can be made in £25 units.

Interest - fixed at the time you buy. You get nothing if you cash in during the first year, then interest is credited at rising rates to the end of the fifth year, averaging for the 40th issue, 5.75 per cent. You will get a letter at the end of the term notifying you what your certificates will earn after that, but it is usually best to cash in then and reinvest the money as the "general extension rate" is usually pretty mean.

Withdrawals usually take eight days.

Tax: all Savings Certificates are free of tax.

Index Linking

We are looking at 'safe' investments. For most people that means something where you put £100 in and are certain to get at least £100 out. But, to adapt a favourite comment by the philosopher C.E. Joad, 'it all depends what you mean by safe.'

Inflation has come down significantly, so it is not the great bogey it once was. But who can say what will happen in the years to come? You could argue that the only really safe investment is one which guarantees that if you put £100 in, you will get back enough money to buy what £100 would have bought at the time you made your investment. The nearest you can get to that sort of guarantee is an investment whose return is linked to the retail price index.

Unless you are a short-term saver, and assuming you have your 'rainy day' money some place where it is easy to get at, it would seem to make sense to have part of your nest egg in Index Linked Savings Certificates. With these, the value of your savings is increased each year in line with the rise in the Retail Price Index, with extra interest added on top. As with the traditional National Savings Certificates, the minimum purchase is £100 and the normal maximum holding is £10,000. They are aimed at the five-year saver, who gets the best deal, and are tax free.

Interest: on top of the index-linking, you get interest for each completed year after the first, averaging, for the sixth issue, 3.25 per cent over the five years. Rates are fixed for the life of your certificates. As with other savings certificates, you cash in with forms available at the post office and it takes about eight days.

Tax: none to pay.

Capital Bonds

These are similar to Savings Certificates, except that the interest is higher and is taxable.

You buy in £100 units at the post office. They are suitable for non tax payers as interest is credited without tax being taken off.

Interest is fixed for five years at the rate when you buy. Series G Bonds pay 7.75 per cent at the full five-year rate.

Withdrawals take about eight days, using forms from the post office. Automatically repaid with the interest after five years.

Tax: has to be paid.

Income Bonds

You can invest anything from £2,000 to £250,000 and you get regular monthly income.Interest - is not fixed, so can rise or fall. August 1993 rates were seven per cent for sums up to £25,000 and 7.25 per cent for larger amounts.

Withdrawals - need to be planned in advance as you have to give three months notice. Only half the interest rate is paid if you withdraw in the first year.

Tax has to be paid if your total income takes you into a tax bracket.

First Option Bonds

These are for lump sums of £1,000 or more (maximum £250,000) which you want to invest for a year or more. Non tax payers may prefer Income Bonds as tax is deducted at the basic rate from First Option Bond interest payments. That is an exception to the general National Savings rule. Interest rates are fixed for 12 months from the date that you buy. At the end of each year, you get a letter telling you what guaranteed rate you will get if you keep the Bond.

Interest is paid at the rate of 4.75 per cent net (equal to 6.34 per cent before deduction of tax) in August 1993. Holdings of £20,000 or more get a bonus of 0.3 per cent net (0.4 per cent gross) each year.

Withdrawals take only a few days and can be done at any time. But the best time is at the anniversary date, otherwise you lose half the interest since the last anniversary date.

Tax is deducted at source. Higher rate payers will have to pay more.

Premium Bonds

A gamble where you cannot lose - but get no interest. Interest at the rate of five per cent is paid by the government and goes straight into the prize pool. Minimum purchase is £100 and you can hold a maximum of £20,000 worth. Each month, around 160,000 prizes are paid, ranging from £50 to £250,000. You have to wait three calendar months before your bonds become eligible for the draw, so the best time to buy is just before the end of a month.

The odds for each £1 bond unit winning a prize are around 15,000 to one in each monthly draw. Statistics suggest that if you hold £1,250 worth you should win a prize each year and with the maximum £20,000 worth you might get 16 prizes in a year. But it is all a matter of how lucky you are - you might win nothing, or a small fortune.

Cashing bonds takes about eight days, using forms from the post office.

Tax: all prizes are tax free - even the big ones.

Children's Bonus Bonds

These are tax-free investments for children and make ideal gifts, with the minimum investment as low as £25. The government is particularly generous with the interest rates on these bonds. Issue E pays the equivalent of 7.85 per cent if held for its full five-year term, all tax free. The maximum holding is, however, limited to £1,000 per child. You buy at a post office, but need to know the child's full name, together with the date and place of birth. The child gets control of the bond on his or her 16th birthday.

Interest is fixed at the time of purchase and, like Savings Certificates, is low in the early years and high at the end (to average out at 7.85 per cent for Issue E).

Withdrawals take about eight working days.

Tax: even if the bond is bought by a parent, there is no tax to pay.

Tax free savings (TESSAs)

Most banks and building societies offer TESSAs. These are the Tax Free Special Savings Accounts. They are best for people with some savings already in hand and who can wait for five years to get the full benefits. But they are also a good way of saving regularly and the interest rates are usually competitive.

You are allowed only one, so it pays to shop around a bit to see who is offering the best rates at the time you start. The rates will in any case vary as they are not normally fixed rate investments.

The special rules allow you to invest up to £3,000 in the first year, followed by £1,800 in each of the next three years and £600 in the last year to make a grand total of £9,000.

Withdrawals - you can withdraw interest if you need the income during the five years, but it is paid after deduction of tax. That is held until the end of the term and if you have drawn no more than the interest, you will have the tax credited back to you. If you withdraw capital, you lose the tax exemption.

Tax tip

Each year the Inland Revenue collects millions of pounds

from people who should not be paying tax - even though it tries not to do this.

Remember: banks and building societies deduct basic rate tax when they credit your interest. If you are sure your income will not exceed your personal allowance (£3,445 in 1993/4) you can fill in an Inland Revenue form at your local bank or society branch to register as a non tax payer and have the interest credited gross (i.e. without tax being taken off first).

If you did not do this, but find at the end of the year that your income was below the allowance level, you can still contact the Inland Revenue and claim back the tax which was deducted.

Note: This concession applies to wives and children who now all have their own personal tax allowance, which covers interest and dividends as well as wages. You cannot, however, use your children as a tax-free zone. If the capital came from the parent only the first £100 of interest escapes tax.

BANKS AND BUILDING SOCIETIES

All banks and building societies offer a wide range of choices to the saver and investor. The big difference used to be the cheque book, but a number of building societies offer cheque book accounts. You can earn a tiny amount of interest on these easy-access, or current, accounts at a lot of banks as well as building societies.

The saver and investor wants more for his money. The general rule is that the more you invest, the better the interest rate which you get. And if you are prepared to lock your money away for set periods, seven days, 30 days, 90 days or sometimes longer, you get a higher rate for that, too.

In most cases, you can get your money out earlier than the notice period, but you will suffer an interest rate penalty. Some of these accounts offer a fixed rate of interest, but most are variable, moving up and down according to the general level of interest rates set by the government.

Building Societies

Building societies are good places for the novice saver, and the not so new, to start building up some capital.

Paid-up share or deposit accounts are the traditional and simplest ones and they have a variety of names. The key feature is that you have access to your money whenever you want it. Interest, however, is low and in some cases you might even have to pay a quarterly charge, perhaps £2.50, if your credit balance falls below £50. There may also be charges for some of the withdrawals from accounts where the balance is less than £250. Few societies make this sort of charge, but the fashion may grow.

Once your balance gets above £500, it pays to start thinking about moving up to another account. At the time of writing, the Halifax paid one per cent on share or deposit accounts, but 4.1 per cent gross (3.08 per cent net) on its Instant Xtra Plus account for deposits of £500 to £2,500. You get a passbook with this sort of account and instant access to your cash. The interest rate rises with the top rate being paid on £25,000 or more.

Some societies offer postal accounts, so that in effect your local branch is the nearest pillar box. Operating by post is cheaper for them than having crowds at their high street branches, so the interest is usually a bit higher, although most want you to deposit £2,500 before opening the account.

If you want monthly income, some accounts offer this. Others credit the interest yearly. Decide what you want and check around to see which account looks best for you.

If you are using one of the higher interest accounts, try to plan ahead for withdrawals. If, for example, it is a 90 day account, try to put in your withdrawal application at least 90 days before you need the cash and in that way you will not suffer an interest rate penalty. One obvious reason for a planned withdrawal is to pay for a holiday. Even if you intend trying for a last-minute bargain you probably know at least three months in advance when you will be going.

Banks

Like the building societies, they have to attract deposits if they are to be able to lend out on mortgages and overdrafts. So they, too, offer savers a whole range of accounts, which they try to keep competitive.

As with the building societies, interest rates are mainly variable and you get the best deals with the biggest deposits and the longest notice for withdrawals. Including special accounts for children and students, Barclays had 13 different accounts to pick and choose from. That is fairly typical of all the banks, so you do need to look around a bit to find the account which suits you best.

For money which is easy to get at, but where interest can range from 2.20 per cent (1.65 net) on modest sums to 3.60 per cent (2.70) for £25,000, most banks offer accounts with names such as "money market" or "higher rate deposit" which pay interest linked to what is obtainable on the London money market. Some of these accounts offer cheque books, others allow immediate transfer to current accounts. Banks also offer 30 day and 90 day accounts, some giving monthly or quarterly interest.

When interest rates are high, you can get some attractive deals by locking money up for longer periods, say two to five or even ten years with banks, building societies, insurance companies and finance houses. But you need to think hard about which way interest rates are likely to move before you tie up your money at fixed rates for long periods.

If you think the general level is more likely to rise than to fall, you would be better off with a variable rate account.

Finance Houses

Some are classed as banks, and even owned by the High Street banks, but if they seek deposits from the public all have to be licensed. They may offer slightly better rates of interest for varying periods. If they are classed as 'banks' they will be covered by the Deposit Protection scheme.

Cash Unit Trusts

Most of the unit trust management groups offer cash unit trusts which are safe enough and give a competitive rate of interest. The management firms run them largely as a place for investors to park money if, for one reason or another, they have sold other units and not yet made up their minds which to buy next. But you can use them as a safe place for lump sums. The managers invest the money in the City's money markets where because of the amounts they invest they can get better rates than you could on your own. The price of the units goes up as interest earned is paid into the fund. The investments are held by trustees who are usually very large banks. See the Long Term Savings chapter.

CHAPTER 3

HOMES

BUYING your own home is one of the biggest investment decisions you'll have to make. Gone are the days when house prices rise day after day. But after allowing for what you'd otherwise be forking out in rent it should prove a sound long term investment.

That's certainly the case if you buy at a competitive price. And right now may well prove one of the best possible times to buy, especially if you're buying for the first time. You'll be benefiting from one of the steepest falls in house prices in living memory.

But it is far from being the first. House prices fell in REAL terms, after allowing for inflation, between 1974 and 1977 and again in the early 1980s. We've now seen an actual drop in asking prices simply because inflation is too low now to camouflage the fall as it did in previous setbacks. Even so, the average home nationally now costs around £63,000 compared with less than £56,000 five years ago. And over 25 years - the life of the typical mortgage- it has risen from a modest £4,400 back in 1968. So don't be put off from buying now, especially if you're buying for the first time.

Mortgages are freely available with banks and building societies offering all sorts of easy start schemes to help you get your first foot on the housing ladder. You'll have little difficulty beating down the price should you find your dream home.

Existing owners may find it harder to sell. But if, like most people, you're after a dearer property you'll save more on the place you're going for than you need to shave off your asking price to finish the deal. Estate agents suggest that the best way to go about it is to clinch a buyer for your home BEFORE making an offer for the one you're after yourself. With house prices recovering slowly there's little risk of being priced out of the market. Some canny folk are selling up, taking a place to rent for the time being ready to grab a bargain when it comes along.

With a fat cash deposit in their pocket from their last home and a firm mortgage offer tucked in their wallets they have the whip hand over any desperate would-be seller.

WHAT CAN I PAY?

Most lenders are prepared to offer you a loan up to 3 times your regular yearly income depending on your age. If you're married or engaged they'll add in one year of your partner's annual income. Or they may be a little more generous and allow you two-and-a-half times your joint income.

Generally speaking they won't allow more because once you start a family that second income may no longer be there.Indeed, many families now struggling to meet their mortgage payments are in difficulty because baby came sooner than they expected wiping out one of their two incomes.

On an income of, say £290 a week, £15,000 a year, you might expect to get a loan of up to £48,750. If your wife was earning £175 a week, £9,000 a year, as well, lenders might go to £60,000. They will normally expect you to put down a ten per cent deposit out of your own savings. But it is possible to get a loan for the full amount, especially on new homes.

BUYING COSTS

Young couples are now paying £45,300 on average for their first home.

And they're putting down a cash deposit of £5,300 and borrowing the remaining £40,000.

At present interest rates that'll cost them about £273 a month to repay.

34

But there are other buying costs to meet as well.

All told you'll need to have put aside at least £1,000 for these on top of your deposit.

First you must pay a VALUATION FEE to the bank or building society for considering your mortgage application. Most of this covers the cost of sending a surveyor to value the place and check that it is worth lending against.

On a £40,000 mortgage it works out at about £125.

You should also have a full STRUCTURAL SURVEY carried out to be sure that the place is sound and worth what they're asking asking for it.

It will let you know whether the wiring or roof need replacing or repairing or whether there's been any subsidence damage.

You need to know that because any insurance you take out on your new home won't cover you against any past damage- even if you only discover it later on.

For a full survey you should allow about £250.

Many lenders offer money saving deals under which the same surveyor carries out both the valuation and your survey at the same time and produce one combined report.

That might cost, say £160.

Fortunately STAMP DUTY has now been removed on homes costing less than £60,000. Above that it works out at one per cent of the purchase price. But that need not worry most first time buyers.

SOLICITOR'S FEES vary considerably and could cost anything from £100 to £300 depending on where you live and which one you use. So shop around and ask for written estimates before choosing one. There's often a saving if you use the same firm as the lender employs for his part of the transaction.

Don't forget to budget for REMOVAL EXPENSES, although many first time buyers do-it-themselves. And there could be re-connection charges to meet for the gas and electricity.

Once you move in you'll need to pay for carpets, curtains, decorating and minor repairs.

WHICH MORTGAGE?

Mortgages are cheap and plentiful right now. There are lots of special deals around, especially if you're buying for the first time. So shop around. Best way to compare them is to find out how much you'll have to repay each month.

But watch out for deals which offer you lower payments now only to bump them up sharply in the next year or two.

That could prove a nasty shock if your pay hasn't improved in the meantime. Or there's been an unexpected addition to the family.

Simplest way to buy your home is with a straight REPAY-MENT mortgage where you pay interest each month on the loan plus a little off the amount borrowed.

Its especially attractive for people who like to see their mortgage debt going down year by year and would like to pay it off sooner rather than later, by, for example stepping up the payments when they can afford to do so.

And it leads to least complications when you move home or if you run into difficulty because you lose your job or become seriously ill.

Make sure, however, that you take out a MORTGAGE PROTECTION INSURANCE POLICY to pay off the loan should you die before the mortgage runs off.

With other schemes you pay the monthly INTEREST only on loan. Instead of paying anything off the loan itself each month you chip in to some sort of savings plan which will eventually pay out enough to clear the loan and, maybe leave you with a nice little extra nest egg on top.

Nowadays most people go for an ENDOWMENT MORT-GAGE where the money is invested in a with-profits life insurance policy.

At an interest rate of 7.99 per cent a £40,000 mortgage would cost you about £273 a month, including the mortgage interest, against about £280 on a straight repayment deal. It should pay out enough in 25 years time to pay off the mort-gage and leave you with a useful tax free cash bonus.

Meanwhile it will clear the mortgage in full should you die before it is paid off. There is the remote chance that if the policy did not make enough profit it might not be quite enough to pay off the mortgage.

And you'd lose money if you had to stop the policy in its early years for any reason - such as being unable to afford to keep up the premiums because you were ill or out of work, for example.

A PENSION MORTGAGE works the same way. In this instance you use part of the tax free lump sum your pension pays out when you retire to clear the mortgage. For about £256 a month a man aged 29 could start a pension plan which could produce a tax free lump sum of over £57,000 at 65 - more than enough to clear the mortgage- plus a pension for life of £21,700 a year.

The return is so much better because you get tax relief on pension contributions but no longer on new life policies.

But using part of your lump sum this way could mean there's less money left to spend on other things when you retire. You can get round that by stepping up your pension contributions to earn a fatter pension all round.

Newest idea is a PEP MORTGAGE. This uses the money you make in one of the Government's new Personal Equity Plans to pay off the loan.

If stock markets boom this method would be the best by far.

But its also the riskiest. For if shares crash there might not be enough to meet the mortgage when it falls due.

FIXED OR VARIABLE?

Having decided which kind of repayment method you choose you must now decide whether you want a mortgage which fluctuates with interest rates generally or is set at a fixed rate for a set period of years.

If you can get one fixed for, say, five years, at a rate well below the current variable one it's hard to resist going for it.

But before you do bear in mind that you might feel like kicking yourself if the ordinary mortgage rate later drops well below what you're paying. Or the chance of a much cheaper fix comes along.

For there are stiff penalties often three to six months interest to pay if you want to pull out of an agreed fix ahead of time.

Against that a fixed rate does give you the certainty of knowing how much you're going to have to pay for years ahead. And you won't be caught out by sudden sharp rises in mortgage charges. But think first of the pros and cons before getting into a fix.

To sum up:

METHODS OF REPAYMENT

REPAYMENT

You pay off the loan together with the interest month by month.

Advantages: Simplest and most flexible. If you run into difficulty it's usually easier to sort something out.

Disadvantages: May work out more expensive in the long run.

INTEREST ONLY: You pay interest only off the loan and make regular payments into an investment plan which is used to pay off the loan at the end of the term.

Most common ones are:

Endowment: where an endowment insurance policy is used to pay off the loan.

Pension: paid off with the tax free lump sum most schemes offer at retirement.

Personal Equity Plan (PEPs for short): paid off with the money the plan makes.

Advantages: If these plans do well they may work out cheaper in the long run.

Disadvantages: Less flexible and if they do badly there may not be enough to clear all the mortgage by the due date.

VARIABLE OR FIXED INTEREST

Most people used to have mortgages where the rates varied with interest rates generally. Now you can get loans at a rate fixed at the outset for one two, five or even 25 years.

Advantages: Makes it easy to budget for years ahead without the danger of your payments doubling overnight.

Disadvantages: Can be big up front fees and you may have no choice over where your insure your home.

Some lenders offer LOW START MORTGAGES. The payments start very low and build up later on. This helps you to afford a mortgage sooner rather than later. It is ideal for someone whose income is expected to improve.

However, you're not fully paying your way in the early years so the debt is actually increasing.

Bad news if your income hasn't improved or circumstances worsen by the time the payments start rising.

So few lenders offer these schemes any more.

ADVICE

There's nowhere you can go for absolutely independent advice on mortgages. Most mortgage lenders sell only their own products or are tied to one outside insurance or investment firm.

Some banks and building societies such as NatWest and the Bradford and Bingley are registered to give independent advice and you could contact a local independent financial adviser by ringing 0483 461 461.

But they are paid out of the commission on the investment products they sell. So bear in mind that they have a vested interest in selling you deals which make commission for themselves or their firms.

We have tried to give you an unbiassed view in this book and we give regular updates in Mirror Money.

HOME HUNTING

Before you begin home hunting talk to your bank or building society manager. It's no good setting your heart on a dream home in some estate agent's window.

So find out how much you can afford to pay first.

Many lenders offer certificates showing how big a loan they've promised to earmark for you. You can show this to estate agents and would-be sellers so they can see you mean business.

Your manager should also be able to give you a few tips about where to look for the right homes in your price bracket in his area.

OLD OR NEW?

NEW HOMES carry certain added bonuses. Builders can

often fix up attractive mortgage deals for you and may help meet the buying expenses for first time buyers.

There'll be little to spend on maintenance and decoration for the first year or two and the house or flat comes with a ten year structural guarantee.

When sales are slack, as they are now, they often throw in things like carpets and curtains for free.

Some starter homes come with fully fitted kitchens including cookers and fridges.

Great if that's what you want. But remember that you'll have to pay for them in the asking price. And when you come to sell them the next buyer might not be that keen on your second hand kitchen equipment.

SECOND HAND homes often come with useful extras such as fitted carpets, an attractive garden, light and bathroom fittings and even some furniture.

And they're usually closer to shops, schools and the station than new homes. But often there are some repairs and maintenance needed right away. And you MUST have a full structural survey.

Anyone who has been a council tenant for at least two years has the RIGHT TO BUY their home- usually at a substantial discount.

This can be mean anything from 32per cent to 60per cent off a council house and as much as 70per cent off a flat.

Ask your town hall for details.

Should you decide to go ahead most banks, building societies, or even your local insurance man will be happy to fix up a mortgage for you and guide you through the maze of paperwork.

INSURANCE

Having bought your home make sure that it is fully insured. The building society may well want to arrange that for you as part of the mortgage deal. Premiums depend upon the rebuilding cost of your home and where it is.

A typical £49,000 home would cost about £98 a year to insure. Strictly speaking the house is yours from the day you exchange contracts so you should really take out insurance then. Don't forget to cover your home contents too. Typical premium is £35 a year for £10,000 of cover. But premiums are much higher in crime ridden areas than in more peaceful places.

MOVE OR IMPROVE?

Once you've been in your home for a while you may find that it is no longer big enough for you or lacks certain amenities.

MOVING house is expensive- all told it can easily cost you anything from £3,000 to £5,000.

IMPROVING your home may look like the cheaper option. But before deciding remember that all too often people who spend a lot doing up their homes still move soon afterwards. That's because they are basically dissatisfied with it and really want a much bigger or better place.

So before turning your home into a building site decide whether you really want to move or improve.

Some improvements are better investments than others.

One which should pay for themselves include:

Installing CENTRAL HEATING, EXTENSIONS for extra bedrooms, larger bathrooms or kitchens and LOFT CONVERSIONS, provided they are well designed and constructed. GARAGES are also worthwhile.

Ones you're unlikely to recoup the cost of when you move include DOUBLE GLAZING, REFITTED KITCHENS and BATHROOMS and LANDSCAPED GARDENS. Attractive improvements, however, should make your home more easily resaleable even if they don't add to the price it will fetch.

If you need to raise the money to pay for improvements the best deal you'll get is to ask your building society or bank to add it to your mortgage. Failing that ask for a home improvement loan.

Finance companies work out much dearer. So do "never-never" deals offered by double glazing and home improvement companies.

Whatever you do don't lose an arm and a leg to a loan shark.

If you can afford to repay the loan quickly you could simply put it on a credit card. This works out quite cheap if you can pay it off in full within a year - see the next chapter.

CASHING IN

Your home should not only prove a sound investment but may even help keep you in your old age.

Easiest way to do this is to sell your home when it becomes too big for you and buy a smaller retirement home which is cheaper and easier to maintain and invest the difference.

But if like many people you prefer to stay put there are many schemes available which allow you to raise money on your home, usually by taking out a fresh mortgage on it.

You can either take a lump sum or use the cash raised to provide an extra pension.

For details of these schemes contact Hinton and Wild, Freepost, Surbiton, Surrey, KT6 7BR. Or ring 081-390-8160.

MORTGAGE REPAYMENT CHART

WHAT A £60,000 MORTGAGE WILL COST YOU...

Source: Halifax Building Society

Interest rate (%)	Endowment	Repayment
15	741.13	690.35
14	697.39	650.59
13	653.63	611.48
12	609.88	573.10
11	566.13	535.85
10	522.38	498.94
9	478.63	463.38
8	434.88	428.99
7	391.13	393.90
6	347.38	364.23
5	303.63	334.11

CHAPTER 4

CREDIT

BACK in the high spending 1980s when greed was supposed to be good few people seemed very bothered about saving money.

The key was to spend as much cash as possible and worry about the bills later.

Banks and building societies were falling over themselves to offer loans and rival money firms from abroad were muscling in on the market with easy credit of their own.

It seemed like the borrowing boom was never going to end. But unemployment and the recession changed all that. Millions of people saw their incomes dry up while the bills kept pouring in. Suddenly the easy terms were looking pretty hard to swallow and the so-called credit revolution turned sour.

Last year debt was the single biggest problem taken to Citizens Advice Bureaux, overtaking social security problems for the first time ever. Bureaux staff handled a record 1,800,000 questions about debts - up by nearly a fifth in just 12 months - and so far this year the problem is showing no sign of going away.

The ways of dealing with debt are discussed in later in the book. But a lot of debt problems can be avoided in the first place by borrowing intelligently.

So what are the right and wrong ways of borrowing

money? Some, like credit cards or agreed overdrafts are perfect if you need a small amount of cash for a short amount of time. Credit cards can be a lot cheaper than bank or other loans for short-term borrowing as there's an interest-free period – which can be up to 56 days – before you incur any charges; also there are no fixing-up fees and no penalty charges if you pay off what you owe sooner than you planned. Other methods of borrowing, such as personal loans or hire purchase, are better suited for larger sums which cannot be repaid so quickly.

The general advice for all of them is to look before you leap - if a debt is going to take several months or even years to clear it is worth taking some time to shop around rather than signing up for the first deal on offer.

CREDIT CARDS

Once upon a time flexible friends were just that. They cost nothing to hold and meant shoppers could go on a spending spree knowing they had up to eight weeks to settle the bill before they paid a penny interest.

Unfortunately times have changed. The card companies cottoned on to the fact that this generosity was costing them a small fortune and set out to find ways of getting something back.

First came annual fees for the privilege of keeping a card. The average charge is now around £10 a year but some are much more costly.

Then the amount of credit on offer was gradually cut back - nowadays if you can't afford to pay off the balance in full each month you'll be hit for interest on everything outstanding - and it will be charged from the day you use the card rather than the day the bill is printed. And the interest-free period on purchases has been sharply reduced by many of the credit card companies.

Credit card interest rates themselves have also proved to be anything but flexible. When bank rates go through the roof so too do credit card interest bills. But when bank rate falls card companies take a long time to reduce their charges - and some never get around to it at all.

Everyone from the Consumers Association to MPs have demanded easier terms but credit card companies have turned a deaf ear. Despite this they are the easiest way to spread a bill over a few pay days and also offer valuable perks which mean canny customers who can afford to pay cash slap their shopping on plastic anyway.

At the top of the list of free advantages of credit cards is purchase insurance, usually giving 100 days free cover against loss or damage to shopping. Travel insurance is also included on most cards promising a lump sum payment if the holder or a member of the family dies or is injured whilst travelling on a holiday paid for with a card. And they can give cover if a tour operator goes bust before a holiday begins. Some cards also give shoppers points depending on how much they spend which can be traded in for free gifts.

Others clock up air miles and so-called 'affinity' cards donate money to a chosen charity whenever holders spend £100 or so. The Royal Society for the Protection of Birds has so far collected more than £1 million from its Co-operative Bank card and the Leeds Permanent building society is in the Guinness Book of Records for handing over a record breaking cheque for £4 million to three charities, the British Heart Foundation, the Imperial Cancer Research Fund and Mencap on behalf of its Visa card holders.

Because these cards cost the banks and building societies so much money they are rarely advertised so customers have to go direct to a charity to ask for an application form.

DO shop around to find a card without an annual fee if you think you can afford to pay off your balance in full each month.

DON'T forget that if you are going to need more time to pay, the key thing is the annual interest rate or APR. Look for the lowest rate around.

DON'T spend more than your credit limit without asking for permission. If you do the card company can demand a higher than usual minimum payment to bring you back into line.

DO remember that new debit cards like Switch, which can carry the Visa symbol, are not credit cards and take money out of a bank account even faster than a cheque. So if you use them when you don't have much cash in your account they can push you overdrawn.

STORE CARDS

If credit card charges look steep then store card costs look like Mount Everest. Many charge well over 30 per cent annual interest even when bank rate is below 10 per cent. It makes them one of the most expensive ways to borrow long term. But if you know you can pay off your balance by the due date they do offer extra benefits like customer discounts, normally around 10 per cent, exclusive shopping evenings and sale previews. Most store cards work like normal credit cards but some, called budget cards, offer a fixed amount of credit in return for regular payments. These are often recommended for youngsters who cannot afford to pay cash for everything but who need to keep their shopping under strict limits.

DO apply for a store card if you've got the cash already and only want to qualify for discounts. DO check if you qualify for a lower interest rate by paying by direct debit from a bank or building society account. DON'T be tempted to spend too much on a store card - most shops accept all the usual Visa or mastercards too so it may be cheaper to use them.

GOLD CARDS

The ultimate status symbol of the 1980s have lost their sparkle now that hard up holders have started looking at the small print and seen how much they cost. Annual interest rates are often lower than on normal cards but the annual fees – often around £60 - are likely to wipe out any savings. Card-holders need to prove they earn enough to be given a card, and they'll probably need all their wages to pay the bill!

DO remember you are paying through the nose just to look flash - ordinary cards make more sense. DON'T forget that swanky 'charge cards' like American Express are quite different to normal credit cards. With these you get unlimited spending power – but you have to pay the bill in full when it comes in rather than spread it over a few months.

OVERDRAFTS

With the recession still clinging on, overdrafts are a fact of life for many people. Massive criticism has forced the big banks to make their charges more obvious - but not to lower them.

Several current accounts offer £100 or so as a free overdraft each month. Beyond this the charges clock starts to tick loud and clear. Authorised overdrafts - where you tell your bank you need to dip further into the red and get given the green light before doing so - are cheapest. Some banks charge a flat fee regardless of how close to your overdraft limit you go, others charge according to the number of cheques you write or how often you use a cashpoint and others may simply charge interest on the amount you borrow.

Anyone who uses authorised or agreed overdrafts often will know how expensive they can be. But the cost fades into nothing compared to the price customers pay for dipping into the red without asking their bank's permission first. These unauthorised overdrafts have soared in price recently - and look set to get even more expensive in the future as the banks try to squeeze every penny they can out of customers.

Offenders will be hit with a flat fee of around £30-£40 for going overdrawn in the first place and will probably be charged another £15 or so for a letter telling them they're in the red. The actual debt - including these fees - will suffer sky high interest and there may be extra charges every time you write a cheque or use a cashpoint machine.

If you're lucky these charges will apply to the times you use your account after you go overdrawn and will stop as soon as you get back within your limit. If you're unlucky your bank may charge you for every transaction made in the previous three months as well.

DON'T go overdrawn without permission. Most banks will agree to an overdraft over the phone if you are in a hurry and have been a good customer in the past. DO keep your manager up to date if you get in trouble with money, If you leave him in the dark he'll hammer you when things go wrong - and there's nothing you can do about it.

DO arrange an overdraft as a safety net if you think there's the slightest chance you might need one, especially before expensive times of the year like Christmas.

DO complain if you think your charges are too high, some banks may cut them if customers shout loud enough but don't hold your breath waiting.

DO ask your bank manager for advice about wiping out an overdraft with a personal loan if you think you're going to be in the red for some time. It might not always pay off but it can keep the cost of borrowing under control.

HIRE PURCHASE

Many shops offer HP or 'easy terms', especially on expensive items like cars, washing machines and televisions. During sale times offers of 'zero per cent credit' are everywhere. These 'buy now pay later' deals are terrific if you can pay the bill when it's due. But the interest rates are hefty if you need extra time.

Catalogue shopping is famous for monthly repayment schemes which let people buy something today and pay for it over the next few months or even years. Fine - as long as the prices are competitive with the shops. But payments spread over longer terms may include hefty charges.

DO demand to know how much you'll have to pay in interest each month to clear a bill if you miss the deadline.

DO put the due date in your diary and pay the debt in time - some HP firms don't send reminders in the hope that customers forget to settle up and have to pay interest.

That's why its always better to get regular payments like these made by your bank for you by standing order or direct debit whenever possible. Indeed many reputable lenders offer lower charges to customers who repay this way because they know the payments will be more certain.

DO ask if you are allowed to repay the debt early without penalty. DON'T forget that on larger items like cars you may be able to haggle for a big discount if you pay with cash rather than use the garage's own credit terms. Do some sums because the total cost of a personal loan on the discount price may be less than a 'zero per cent credit deal' on the full price.

PERSONAL LOANS

On offer for everything from car buying to home improvements personal loans can be picked up from almost all banks and buildings societies as well as shops and other finance houses. Once you've had a loan agreed it is as good as having cash in your pocket - so you can haggle in the high street for a bargain.

Most personal loans have a fixed rate of interest which is set on the day the loan is taken out. You'll have a choice of payments with or without insurance which promises to cover the debt if you die, have an accident, lose your job or are too ill to work. This can be a valuable benefit though the cost varies widely, so, as usual, it is worth shopping around. Anyone who thinks there may be anything at all unusual about their health or job should read the small print on the policy before signing up as many do not cover self employed people or workers on short term contracts.

Check there are no hidden fees for setting the loan up. Watch out for 'variable' rate loans, the monthly repayments here will go up and down with other interest rates and you could be caught short if your payments increase.

Most smaller loans are called 'unsecured' which means the lender cannot take the borrower's possessions if they default on the repayments. The opposite, a secured loan is usually tied to a house and if borrowers stop making their payments the lender has the right to sell the house to get their money back. The interest rate is usually lower on secured loans but they can be dangerous if you think there is any chance you'll hit trouble paying it off.

DO shop around before applying for a loan. Rates vary widely along the high street. Check the monthly and total costs before signing up and compare it with rival quotes.

DON'T refuse insurance just to save money but do read

the small print before deciding to take it especially if you are self employed or in bad health. DON'T forget that youngsters may get discounts if parents agree to act as 'guarantor' for their payments. Ask for details.

DO check if you'll have to pay a penalty for repaying the loan early.

DON'T get distracted by 'free' offers with loans. A car alarm may sound worth having but it may only be on offer because the lender knows its rates are too high and that no-one would even look at its loan if it didn't have a gimmick.

LOAN SHARKS

A mass of new laws and rules have been set up in recent years to make money lending as fair and safe as possible. But the crooks are still out there - and they tend to prey on those who reckon they won't be given a loan anywhere else.

The Office of Fair Trading reports annual percentage rates in the thousands of percent, and the rumours that kneecaps get broken if you miss a few payments are not far from the truth.

Do remember the old rule that if something sounds too good to be true then it probably is.

DO get an expert to look over the paperwork before you sign. If you are in any doubt, Citizens Advice Bureaux should be able to run a quick check.

DO worry if you are offered cash by an outfit you've never heard of.

DO check your lender has an up to date Consumer Credit Licence before agreeing to take a loan. The Office of Fair Trading in London will look through its records for a small fee.

DON'T think that just because a high street bank or building society has turned you down that your only choice is to go to a backstreet lender.

CREDIT UNIONS where a few like-minded people club together to form a mini-bank may be able to help. The Association of British Credit Unions is on 0695 314444.

DO remember that if you think the interest rate you're paying is too high you can go to court under the Consumer

Credit Act to get it lowered. Local Trading Standards Offices in the phone book are first ports of call for advice.

VISA INTEREST RATES

	Monthly %	APR Purchase %	APR Cash %
ROBERT FLEMING/SAVE & PROSPER (£12 annual fee)	1.00	14.8	16.1
BANK OF SCOTLAND (£10 annual fee)	1.63	22.6	24.5
BARCLAYCARD (£10 annual fee)	1.65	22.9	24.8
COOPERATIVE BANK (£12 annual fee)	1.90	26.8	29.4
COOPERATIVE BANK (£12 annual fee) (minimum direct debit option)	1.70	23.9	26.4
COOPERATIVE BANK 'Robert Owen' VISA Card Amount spent per month			
Under £100	2.20	29.8	32.4
£100–£300	1.95	26.9	28.6
£300+	1.70	22.4	24.9
FIRST DIRECT VISA (£10 annual fee)	1.60	22.2	24.0
GIROBANK (£12 annual fee)	1.69	23.7	25.6
HALIFAX (£10 annual fee)	1.69	23.5	25.4
LEEDS PREMANENT (£12 annual fee)	1.75	24.6	26.5
MIDLAND VISA (£10 annual fee)	1.65	23.1	25.0
NATIONAL PROVINCIAL	1.65	21.6	21.6
NATWEST VISA (£12 annual fee)	1.70	23.9	23.9
NATWEST 'Primary' VISA (£6 annual fee - £500 Fixed Credit Limit)	1.80	25.3	25.3
ROYAL BANK OF SCOTLAND VISA (£10 annual fee)	1.69	23.5	23.5
TSB TRUSTCARD	1.74	22.9	23.4
YORKSHIRE BANK	1.75	23.1	23.7

MASTERCARD INTEREST RATES

	Monthly %	APR Purchase %	APR Cash %
ROBERT FLEMING/SAVE & PROSPER (£12 annual fee)	1.00	14.6	16.1
BANK OF SCOTLAND (£10 annual fee)	1.63	22.6	24.5
BARCLAYS MASTERCARD (£10 annual fee)	1.65	22.9	24.8
CLYDESDALE ACCESS (£10 annual fee)	1.69	23.5	23.5
LLOYDS ACCESS (£12 annual fee)	1.60	22.4	24.3
MIDLAND ACCESS (£12 annual fee)	1.65	23.1	25.0
NATWEST ACCESS (£12 annual fee)	1.70	23.9	23.9
NATWEST MASTERCARD (£12 annual fee)	1.65	23.1	23.1
ROYAL BANK OF SCOTLAND ACCESS (£10 annual fee)	1.69	23.5	23.5
TSB MASTERCARD	1.74	22.9	23.4
OTHER			
AMERICAN EXPRESS OPTIMA (£10 annual fee)	1.66	24.2	26.2

Information provided by Save & Prosper

HOW THE STORES COMPARE

STORE	ACCOUNT TYPE	PAYMENT METHOD	APR
Burton	Option	Direct Debit	26.8%
		Other Means*	29.8%
Dixons/Currys	Budget	Direct Debit	29.8%
		Other Means	34.4%
Kingfisher		Kitchens	24.9%
		Conservatories	19.9%
B&Q	Option		29.4%
Comet	Budget	Direct Debit	29.4%
		Other Means	32.9%
John Lewis			19.5%
Littlewoods	Option	Direct Debit	26.8%
		Others Means	34.8%
Marks & Spencer	Option	Direct Debit	22.4%
		Other Means	25.3%
Sears	Option	Direct Debit	29.8%
		Other Means	32.8%
Selfridges	Option	Direct Debit	23.6%
		Other Means	26.8%

*Cash or cheque. Source: Retail Credit Group

The cheapest credit cards are issued by:
Save & Prosper 21.3 APR
National and Provincial 21.6 APR
First Direct 22.2 APR
Bank of Scotland 22.6 APR
National and Provincial and Save & Prosper don't charge an annual fee.

STORE	APR AUG 1993	APR SEPT 1992	APR SEPT 1990	%POINTS FALL SINCE SEPT 1990
INTEREST RATES (APR) ON STORE CARDS				
BASE RATES	6.0	10.0	15.0	9.0
SELFRIDGES With direct debit Without direct debit	23.8 26.8	26.8 29.8	29.8 32.9	6.0 6.1
WALLIS,WAREHOUSE With direct debit Without direct debit	28.8 29.9	29.8 32.9	32.9 38.4	4.1 8.5
DIXONS With direct debit Without direct debit	29.8 34.4	32.9 37.6	36.8 41.7	7.0 7.3
MARKS & SPENCER With direct debit Without direct debit	22.4 25.3	26.0 26.8	29.8 34.4	7.4 9.1
JOHN LEWIS Without direct debit	19.5	23.8	23.8	4.3
BURTON GROUP With direct debit Without direct debit	26.8 27.3	30.6 33.7	30.6 33.7	3.8 6.4
HABITAT With direct debit Without direct debit	27.5 30.6	29.8 32.9	30.6 32.9	3.1 2.3
NEXT Club 24	30.0	36.0	36.0	6.0
BARCLAYCARD	22.9	28.5	27.8	4.9

CHAPTER 5

INSURANCE

IF A frozen pipe bursts and floods your home, could you claim on insurance to have it re-decorated and re-furnished? If you were burgled, would you be compensated to replace what was stolen? If you broke your leg abroad on a ski-ing holiday, could you afford to pay the medical bills? If you died suddenly, would your family have enough cash to keep them going as if you were still around?

Accidents happen every day. Almost everyone has been hit by some kind of disaster or knows someone who was. Cars crash, holidays are cancelled, fires break out, people lose their belongings, their jobs, their health, and sometimes their lives.

Insurance is all about taking cover against the risks which could make you worse off. It is supposed to be your cash investment against a disaster, to make good any losses you suffer. But because these days, the higher the risk, the higher the cost of insurance, it is up to you to decide what you can afford as well as whether you can afford to be without it.

The cost of some kinds of insurance has rocketed since the 1980s, so shopping around and taking steps to make yourself less of an insurance risk have never been more important.

And don't forget that if you ever have to make a claim the onus is on YOU to prove that your loss was as much as you say.

So keep receipts and valuations, even of the little things that mean a lot. Take photos of your most treasured possessions; list the serial numbers of your television, camera and video recorder, and anything else.

HOME CONTENTS

One in four people has no insurance on home contents, and thousands more try to keep the costs down by insuring for too little. But being under-insured is just as dangerous as having no insurance at all. If you had to claim, the insurance company could reduce the amount or may even decide not to pay anything.

Most home contents policies are now on a new-for-old basis, which means you are paid the full cost of repairing or replacing missing or damaged items. Indemnity cover costs less because it allows for wear and tear of the item, so pays you a smaller amount depending on how long ago you bought it. However, the problem with indemnity cover is that it may not pay enough to buy a new or even second-hand replacement.

Policies vary but generally include personal effects and valuables up to certain limits. If you want them protected outside the home, you will have to ask for 'all-risks' cover to be included, which can be very expensive, depending on the value of items such as cameras, binoculars, cam-corders and jewellery.

Read the small print to find out what is not covered. If you own a word-processor or fax machine, for instance, you may have to insure them separately. And if you've splashed out on a television or computer for each of the kids, find out if they are all covered. You may find there's a limit.

Most premiums are now worked out on your postcode. If you live in an area where claims have gone through the roof, you can expect to pay a high premium for cover. Computer technology helps insurance firms to keep track of risk-prone areas. But they won't all have the same opinion of every area. It's the number of claims each company must meet that makes the difference. So your job is to find an insurer who has a low claim rate in your area and sets premiums within your price range.

One of the big changes on contents policies is the terms of cover on matching sets or pairs of items in your home. Years ago, if one part of a three-piece suite was damaged, your insurer would take the undamaged items and give you money to buy a completely new suite. That no longer happens. These days the insurer pays for the damaged item only, and you can either hope to match it up or find the rest of the cash for a new suite.

The same goes for carpets. There's no chance of replacing a fitted carpet throughout the home if the damage was confined to one room, as in the past. You'll only be able to claim enough to replace the damaged carpet, even if you can no longer find the same shade.

Some policies are index-linked to help keep your cover up to date. It means that the level of cover goes up in line with the Retail Price Index, so you don't have the bother of trying to work out whether you're under-insured. There are also price packages with set premiums based on the number of bedrooms in your home.

This kind of package deal makes sure you don't set the insured sum too low. But you could be paying too high a premium if you don't own the amount specified in the package. To work out how much your belongings are worth, go through your home room by room, not forgetting the garage, shed and garden totting up what you can. You may be surprised at how asset-rich you are.

If you're renting, check with your landlord who owns what. But don't pay over the odds if you own a modest amount. There are a few companies which cover small amounts for people in bedsits, digs and small flats.

Nowadays insurance companies insist on security locks on doors and windows to reduce the risk of burglary. If you are renting, you should discuss with the landlord who is responsible for fixing your locks.

Crime rate studies show that a home burgled once is twice as likely to be broken into again. That makes it difficult for uninsured burglary victims to arrange cover for the future. Insurers may either refuse cover until you move to another address or charge a much higher premium than normal. They will also want to check your home security. The problem is that thieves assume the owners will replace the stolen items and will plan to return for a second helping.

Burglary only accounts for a fraction of the premium. The

rest is for fire, accidental and weather damage. Most policies have a limit on what they will pay out for a single valuable personal possession, excluding furniture, so you must specify any item which is worth more. Otherwise, if it is lost or stolen, the most you'll get is the single item limit set by your insurers. Check if any equipment you take to work or borrow from your employer to work at home is covered by insurance if it is stolen.

Another common mistake is forgetting to top up your policy when you inherit or buy something extra for the home. A few companies give special cover for people with a valuable painting or piece of antique furniture, and the cover usually includes depreciation in value if the insured item is damaged and worth less after being repaired.

There are several ways you may qualify for a discount on insurance premiums. Most insurance companies offer a discount if you live in a registered Neighbourhood Watch area, if you have secure locks, bolts and a burglar alarm, and if you opt to pay a larger excess on any claim.

A few are beginning to offer a no-claims discount but the largest number operate discounts for over-55s based on the theory that older people are more safety-minded and are often at home at the times burglaries usually occur.

BUILDINGS

The lender helping you to buy your home will insist you have buildings insurance. After all, it is in the lender's interest to protect his investment until the mortgage is repaid and the home is finally all yours.

However, once the deeds are finally in your hands, don't be tempted to let the buildings insurance slide. It may seem a large expense but it's still worth it if your roof tiles blow away in a storm, the chimney comes down in a gale or a tree crashes through the greenhouse.

Weather damage, and in particular, subsidence caused by a series of hot, dry summers, is an expensive problem and the cost of tackling the repairs out of your own pocket may be more than you could bear.

The amount you insure your home for is based on how

much it would cost to rebuild, not on its market value. Some areas are more expensive to insure than others, depending on the type of location. As morsels of Britain's coastline break off and plop into the sea, the owners of clifftop homes have to face a rising cost in premiums, providing they can get insurance at all.

Central heating, double glazing, paths and garages are all covered, but watch out for exclusions, like storm damage to fences. You're generally covered for damage if your TV aerial or satellite dish caused it when it blew down, but it's likely you'll have to claim for the aerial or dish under your home contents policy. Some insurance companies have changed their minds about covering satellite dishes lately, so check the small print.

There will also be excesses, especially for subsidence, which means you pay the first few hundred pounds of the repair bill.

Subsidence mostly affects homes built on clay soil. The checks to prove it may last for months before underpinning can take place. Some parts of the country are more at risk of subsidence because of the soil content, and the homeowners face high premiums and a much higher excess than before because of the increasing number of claims.

If your premiums go up, don't be too quick to change your insurance company. Be absolutely sure your home has no telltale cracks which point to possible subsidence. If you have to claim for subsidence later, your new insurer may argue that the problem started before you joined them. As it takes so long for the symptoms of subsidence to appear, you may have a hard time proving them wrong.

An insurance company would still be liable for recurring problems if they opted for repairs which failed to correct the original trouble and fell short of the remedy suggested by engineers acting on your behalf.

When you buy a property, make sure you jot down details of the vendor's building insurance policy and their new address. Then ask your solicitor to get an undertaking from theirs to support any future claim against their building insurance if subsidence occurs not long after you move in.

If you need to claim for weather damage after a flood or storm, don't have repairs done before you get the go-ahead from your insurer. Most insurance firms have a hotline for homeowners to call after storm damage. They'll advise on what steps to take to prevent the risk of further damage by covering holes in roofs or windows with plastic or tarpaulin, and you should be able to recover the cost of this on your insurance policy.

But to make a successful claim, your insurers will want to be certain that you kept your home maintenance up to scratch. They won't pay out for a chimney which blew down if it was unsteady before the storm, or for gutters and drain-pipes which had come loose from their moorings.

The cost of your claim could also be reduced if you don't obtain a written estimate. But not all estimates are free so ask if there's a charge, and ask for the estimate to be broken down into hourly labour rates and materials, so you know what you're paying for. Make sure it includes the clearing of debris.

YOUR LIFE

Surveys show around one in five people has no personal life cover and only five percent of those who do have enough to provide their families with the income they would need to cope with the bills.

Life cover is important for several reasons. If you have debts, such as a mortgage or bank loan, or you're buying furniture or car on credit, your family may be able to pay what is owing with cash from your life policy if the worst happened.

Secondly, a life policy is another way of saving regularly, paying you back the premiums, sometimes with some interest, if you survive beyond a certain date.

There are many different types of life cover. A whole life policy guarantees an agreed sum when you die. The premiums you pay depend on the amount payable at your death, as well as your age, health and job. If you want to stop paying premiums when you retire the premiums will have to be set higher during your working years.

The cheapest life policy is term assurance. An agreed sum is paid only if you die within a certain time set out in the policy. It's just about the best choice for a young couple with children who need a lot of cover. The premiums cost less because there's a good chance you will outlive the term set in the policy, in which case you won't get any cash back. But it gives you peace of mind knowing that the mortgage and any other debts will be paid if you did not survive that long.

Endowment cover is used for saving a particular sum over a long term which could be anything from 10 to 25 years. The date for the policy to pay out your lump sum is written into the policy. But if you die before reaching it, the full sum is paid to your family and no more premiums are paid.

A with-profits policy pays a bonus at the end but costs a little more in premiums than one without profits and you won't know exactly how much the bonus will be.

Or there's the choice of a unit-linked policy, tied in to investments on the stock market. The amount you get at the end depends on the success of the investment when the time comes to pay out. Most of these plans offer a minimum amount if you die early.

Almost any major financial step you take will involve some life cover. For example, you may be asked to take out a mortgage protection policy when you take out a mortgage. The policy will pay back your loan if you die before it's repaid. And most pension schemes, including personal pensions, may include a small amount of life cover which is paid to your family if you die before you start to claim the pension.

HEALTH

Ill-health is another one of those things we think happens to other people. But about one in four men over 45 is off work through ill health for six months or more, and women are even more likely than men to be sick for a long time.

Few families could manage to pay their regular bills if they had to fall back on state handouts for several months.

Permanent health insurance, sometimes known as income

protection, pays a weekly or monthly benefit while you are sick or disabled and unable to work. Payments could last up to retirement, if necessary, but only start after you've been off work for several weeks. Most policies don't pay in the first month and the longer you're prepared to wait before drawing an income, the cheaper your premiums.

Many policies only pay if you cannot work at all, while others pay up if you can't go back to your normal job. If your ill health means a drop in salary when you go back to work, some policies will pay a reduced benefit to make up the loss in your earnings. But before paying any claim, the insurance company will want a medical report from a doctor of their choice.

CARS

Security is the name of the game since increasing car crimes have forced insurers to put up premiums. You can save pounds on car insurance if you buy anti-theft devices that immobilise the engine to prevent it from being driven away, have windows etched with a serial number, and get a car alarm.

Insurance firms now have a lot more group ratings aimed at making premiums fairer for cars which are similar but not the same as each other. An average motorist should find the new ratings make no difference or leave him better off.

The cars involved in most claims - powerful racy models and hot hatches - are the more expensive to insure. So it pays to stick to lower-rated cars until you've built up the maximum no-claims discount.

You can make savings by limiting your cover to named drivers or only those over 25; increase your excess on any claim; ask a garage or motoring organisation how you can make your car more secure.

Car-owners with comprehensive cover who restrict the number of drivers may not be able to claim if someone else gets behind the wheel and has a prang. The cover is limited to third party only, in that case. It will pay for damage to the other person's car but not yours.

Your insurers will want to know the age, job, driving experience and driving record of anyone likely to drive your car, and if you want to use the car for work, you must say so.

You can protect a no-claims discount by paying an extra premium. That usually allows you two claims over three or five years without loss of discount.

Your insurance provides the minimum cover required by law if you want to take your car abroad to another EC country. But it will not include theft or damage to your car, and may not completely cover your liability to other people. If you let your insurers know about your trip in advance they can extend your cover to most holiday spots. You will also need a Green Card, available from your insurers, as proof of your insurance cover.

HOLIDAYS

One in 12 holidaymakers claim on their holiday insurance. About half the claims are for holiday cancellation because of illness, loss of job or a death in the family. A quarter are for medical expenses, and around 12 per cent are for loss of belongings.

Insurance companies can refuse claims for various reasons. Some are turned down because the policyholder did not get in touch within the time limit specified in the small print.

Others may question your claim that you lost that expensive camera or necklace on holiday if you cannot prove you owned them in the first place. Without a receipt or a photo of the missing items they have no proof they even existed.

The onus is also on the policyholder to keep an eagle eye on their belongings. Leaving your luggage in a taxi that drives off with it while you've popped into the hotel for someone to help you could be construed as negligence and you may not be compensated for your loss.

Being on holiday does not mean you can afford to relax so much that you let your guard down. Cameras and transistor radios should not be left on a poolside deckchair or a train seat to reserve your place while you go for a drink.

Some policies will pay out for items stolen from the glove compartment or boot of a car but not for anything lying around on the seats in full view of a passing opportunist thief. And if you wish to leave your things on a coach seat, check that your driver will lock the doors or stay with it when you stop for lunch.

The 'all-risks' cover on your home contents policy may be more generous than run-of-the-mill package holiday insurance. The low limit on some policies may be less than your luggage is worth.

It is also worth checking on the limits of medical expenses. Medical care can be very expensive in some parts of the world and may not be fully covered under a package policy. You may want to take out additional cover through the tour operator or an insurance broker.

Make sure you get what you want. Some policies may refuse cover for illnesses connected with pregnancy. Most will exclude covering activities which seem risky, such as hang-gliding, rock-climbing or ski-ing. Ask your travel agent about arranging a special policy.

PETS

Half the homes in Britain have pets and they cost us millions to look after them. Vet bills alone are a heavy drain, but there's no limit to the number of illnesses and injuries a standard pet policy will cover.

Insurance won't cover vaccinations, pregnancy, neutering and illnesses diagnosed before you took out the policy, or after the pet reaches a certain age.

But you'll get a lump sum if your pet is killed in an accident or dies from an illness as long as it is below the age set by the insurer.

Policies pay boarding fees for your pet if you have to go into hospital, and the cost of advertising a missing pet, plus the reward offered for its return. You'll also be compensated if it is not found.

TOP TEN PAY-OUTS

£50 a month invested for 25 years by a 29-year-old man

General Accident:	£110,452
Standard Life:	£105,897
Commercial Union:	£105,266
Tunbridge Wells:	£104,648
Friends Provident:	£103,733
Royal London:	£103,529
Legal & General:	£103,316
Scottish Amicable:	£103,030
Scottish Life:	£102,975
Clerical Medical:	£102,644
Average pay-out:	£93,423
Lowest pay-out:	£73,418

Source: Money Management

CHAPTER 6

YOU AND YOUR CAR

EVERYBODY wants to have a car, whether it is a snappy little sports model with an open top and stereo system or a family run around for supermarket trips and taking the kids to school. But the cost of owning and running wheels is going to be your biggest expense after your mortgage so the message is: Think carefully about all the costs involved.

Biggest item particularly with a new car is likely to be the way it falls in value each year as it gets older. Basing its figures on driving the average of 10,000 miles a year the AA estimates depreciation for a new car with engine capacity up to 1,000cc is £833.50 in a year, for 1001 to 1400cc £1,253.13, for 1401 to 2000cc £1752.02, for 2001 to 3000cc it is £3,288.88 and for 3001 to 4500cc that comes to £4,287.

Then there is insurance, the licence disc and if you join for the breakdown and other services it gives AA or RAC subscriptions of around £64 a year.

For 10,000 miles a year all that works out at 16.5p a mile for a car up to 1,000cc, 22.45p for 1,001 to 1400cc, and 29.09p for 1401 to 2000cc jumping to 49.73p and 60.21p for the next two categories.

Add up the cost of petrol, oil, tyres, servicing and repairs and replacements and you come to running costs rising from 13.03p a mile to 14.32p, 16.50p, 23.80p and 28.85p. If you can do your own servicing you could save 1.2p to 2.45p a mile and more if you can do your own repairs. But if you are thinking about an average car of 1.4 litre capacity doing 10,000 miles a year you need to think in terms of it costing around 30p a mile

The AA table shows costs per mile for 10,000 miles use in a year coming out at 29.48p for up to 1,000cc, 36.77p for 1001 to 1400cc, 45.59p for 1401 to 2000cc, 73.53p for 2001 to 3000cc and 89.06p for 3001 to 4500cc.

BUYING A NEW CAR

Check the cost of finance. Not too many of us can walk into the showroom and write out a cheque for a new car although if you can use savings that is the cheapest way of financing it particularly now that interest rates on bank and building society deposits have come down.

Banks and some building societies offer car loans or personal loans which can be used for buying a car.

A loan secured on your house may be cheaper but the house will be at risk if things go wrong for you.

Hire purchase is usually secured on the car. Your dealer will have a number of finance packages. Check around to see what deals are on offer at the time.

Work out which you can afford each month, bearing in mind the insurance and running costs and see which package suits you best. The APR (annual percentage rate) is the best way of comparing the various plans but look also to see if you are asked for an arrangement fee. Lenders like you to take out a protection plan for your loan – insurance to cover payments usually for up to 12 months if you are unable to work because of sickness or accident or are made redundant for no fault of your own after your loan has been in force for 60 days.

Here is one example: The Midland bank offers 17.3 per cent APR for loans over £3,000 (19.4 for smaller amounts) which with a loan protection plan could cost £87.67 a month over 60 months and, over the whole period, add up to a total of £5,295.96.

Without protection the same loan would cost £73.06 a month and a total repayment of £4,383.30.

But before you sign up it is important to compare as many

finance offers as possible including asking your bank about an overdraft because the variations could add up to several hundred pounds over the loan period.

Loans are normally on offer for 12, 24 , 36 , 48 and 60 months. If you go for the shortest period which your budget will allow you will obviously pay less in the long run.

If you take out a long running loan remember that if you want to pay it off early you will probably have to pay a hefty penalty. A conventional overdraft would cost an arrangement fee but you would be able to pay it off whenever you like.

Check the warranty offered. Does it cover three years or only one? And how much of the car is covered? Read the small print.

Think about depreciation. You will be wanting to sell the car at some time so find out if the model you fancy has a good record for reliability and is likely to depreciate less than others. Choose a popular colour. Bright red or white are current favourites.

Haggle. It is always worthwhile seeing if you can strike a deal under the list price particularly towards the end of the year when the quieter winter period is starting. Then see if you can persuade the dealer to put in a better radio. Try for a discount even if you are offered finance at nought per cent or some other particularly cheap rate. Always do your haggling BEFORE you start negotiating the finance.

Part exchange. It is almost certainly a myth that you get a better deal for your old car if you part exchange for a new one.

The dealer will want to make a profit on both of them. Part exchange is convenient but if you can afford the time and trouble you should get more by selling privately.

Check the asking prices for similar cars in your local paper, remembering that is not necessarily the price you will get and compare with what the dealer would offer.

BUYING SECOND HAND

It seems obvious but before you set out you should give a lot of thought to what car you need. You don't want a big car built for long distance cruising if you are going to use it mainly in town centre traffic. Think about such things as petrol consumption, maintenance bills and depreciation.

The world is full of people who will give advice on buying a used car. But in general the old rule of money applies – you get what you pay for.

With a used car however you have to be particularly careful, especially if you are not going to an established reputable dealer.

You may try to depress a private seller into lowering the price by taking a friend along to walk round the car sneering at it and kicking the tyres.

But it is better to pay for an opinion from a qualified mechanic or the AA or RAC. AA charges range from £95 to £279 depending on the make of car for an inspection lasting up to two hours and a report highlighting faults and possible problems.

If you think you know enough about cars to form your own opinion, write out a check list and tick it off as you go over the vehicle.

Special points to note are: rust – look at the door edges, joints, suspension damper mountings and under the car. Remember bubbles in the paint probably indicate rust about to break through. Take a magnet with you in case you think a hole has been patched up. The magnet will not stick to plastic.

Tyres – uneven wear could indicate a mechanical defect. Each tyre should have at least one mm of tread across three quarters of its width.

Switches – check they all work.

Brakes – do they work without judder and will the handbrake hold on a hill?

Clutch – should work smoothly and not slip . Check for slipping in high gear.

Steering – too much free movement of the steering wheel suggests mechanical wear.

Oil pressure – the oil light should go out as soon as the engine is running. Look also at the battery, wiring , hydraulic system, cooling system and exhaust.

Look along the side of the car for any signs that it may have been in a crash. If buying from a dealer ask him : he should tell you.

Go for a test drive with the radio switched off so that you can hear all the noises the car makes. Brake fairly hard when it is safe to do so and see if the car pulls to one side or shudders.

Before you start, check the oil – a coffee colour indicates problems and so does a dark brown colour in the radiator water.

BEWARE THE CROOKED DEALER

Buying from a private seller should mean a lower price than from a dealer, but if the car falls apart on the way home that will be your bad luck.

Some doubtful dealers advertise as if they were private sellers. When you ring up be a bit vague and don't name the car.

If it is a dealer with several dodgy motors he will have to ask which one you want. If there are holes in the dashboard the car may have been a taxi.

Go straight home if the dealer can't show you the log book – the V5 Department of Transport registration document. Make sure that the numbers on the log book match the Vehicle Identification Number under the bonnet and on the bodywork. The AA suggests you avoid personalised number plates from Northern Ireland which always contain the letter I such as GIL or BIL as it is difficult to trace the history of cars carrying these plates.

If a well used car has low mileage be suspicious. Legally a dealer should check the mileage with one of a number of specialised companies who make inquiries or say he cannot guarantee the mileage.

THE LOGBOOK

You have checked all the details on the log book and bought the car and now you MUST make sure the seller sends the tear off slip to the DVLC (Driver and Vehicle Licensing Centre) to confirm legal ownership has changed.

And contact the DVLC yourself, sending the top part of the form to notify them that you are the new "keeper" of the car.

Remember: This does NOT ensure that the car has no outstanding loans on it. You can check with HP Information who keep information on hire purchase, personal loans, rental agreements and so on and also whether a car has been reported stolen, written off by an insurance company or had its licence number changed recently. The inquiry costs £15 which you can pay by quoting your credit card number to get an immediate answer over the telephone.

They get their information from the finance companies, insurance companies, police and the DVLC and this is as accurate as they and their suppliers can make it.

The phone number is 0722 413434.

THE PRICE

Check with one of the used car guides which you can buy at a newsagent as well as looking at local advertised prices. The guides give retail and trade prices to show you some ball park figures. If you are buying from a dealer and not trading in another car expect to get at least ten per cent off his first asking price.

If you are buying from a private seller try not to pay the top retail price indicated in the guides as these will include a profit for the dealer. Run your eye down the prices year by year and note when the gap between retail and trade widens noticeably.

That will be the year the dealer expects to have to sort out some problems before he sells the vehicle. Remember there are lots of used cars on offer and the dealers want to sell them. So check around and haggle .

WARRANTIES

Ask about the warranties offered by your dealer. Compare them as well as the cars. One of the best was organised by Vauxhall for its dealers under the banner Network Q . This means the car is given 114 checks and sold with a free 12 month warranty for mechanical and electrical components specified (items classed as "consumables" which you would expect to replace in routine maintenance are not included).

The scheme covers cars up to five years old with no more than 60,000 miles on the clock. You can usually pay to extend the warranty for another 12 or 24 months.

Ford dealers will quote for A1 Mechanical Breakdown insurance but other dealers have warranties of their own. Costs can range up from £150 for first year cover to £600 or so for extended two year cover depending on the car.

AUCTIONS

These are really for people who know what they are doing. The cars may be hard driven company fleet cars or something which has been standing for weeks on a dealer's forecourt and he cannot sell it. You should be able to save at least ten per cent by buying at an auction, but you have to pay straight away by cash or bankers draft. The car is then yours with little come back. If you insist on trying your luck at an auction go to one or two to get the feel of things before you take the plunge.

See how easy it is to have a look at the car before the auction starts and whether you are given any chance to cancel the deal (usually within an hour or two) if you find some major hidden defect.

You will need to make sure your insurance covers you for driving it away.

INSURANCE

It's the law that you have to have at least third party insurance which means your insurer will pay for damage you cause to someone else if it is your fault. With this sort of cover you pay for the damage to your own car unless you can establish the accident was the other driver's fault.

There are something over 18 million private cars on the road and the insurance industry reckons some five per cent of them are not insured. If you are hit by someone without insurance you can claim some compensation from a bureau set up by the insurance companies but if it is a case of hit and run and you don't know whether the culprit was insured or not because you do not know who he is they will not pay.

The other form of insurance is fully comprehensive which costs something like twice as much. With this policy your company will pay for the damage to both cars if it is your fault. The "knock for knock" agreement started in the early 1950s under which the companies agreed to pay for damage to their own insured vehicles seems on the way out. This is because more people are going for third party only to save paying higher premiums and because the direct selling companies who look like winning 20 to 25 per cent of the market within the next five years have not joined.

The basic advice is: check around. This is a highly competitive industry. Get quotes from one or two brokers plus one or two of the direct selling companies and the AA which insures with a panel of big companies.

But don't just look at the premium price. Consider the service you get and the "excess"- which is the amount of each claim which you have to pay yourself. Check how much you can reduce the premium by agreeing to pay more of the damage yourself . Look at the details of the no claim bonuses which you can accumulate and think about paying a bit extra to protect the bonus if you have to make a claim.

Some insurers bump up the premiums or the excess if you are living in a high crime or high claim area. Teenagers are reckoned to be three times more likely to have accidents than more experienced drivers, so have to pay more. An 18 year old may be asked for a £1,000 annual premium. Adding a youngster to a family policy could still cost £500 and he or she will not be building up their own no claims bonus.

Whatever people say about women drivers, some companies like them and will charge a bit less.

All drivers hate the way premiums have been going up year by year. But in 1992 the industry took in the premiums of £5,700 million and with almost one car in three getting involved in an accident paid out £6,240 million.

The total damage probably cost more than that as many drivers with good bonuses choose to pay modest bills themselves rather than lose the bonus or have it reduced.

If you have an accident, do the sums. Look at what you will have to pay through the excess and how much you will lose if your bonus is cut.

If your car is stolen or becomes a write-off after a crash remember comprehensive cover should get you a cheque big enough to buy a car comparable with the one you lost. If you don't think the company is offering enough – argue.

OVERSEAS

If you take your car overseas you need to carry evidence of insurance with you and also your driving licence in case you get involved in an accident.

A UK insurance certificate usually gives you only the legal

third party limit overseas.The green card extends your comprehensive cover to other countries.

If the companies make a charge it is usually modest and some will give one green card a year free covering you for up to 30 days.

If you want break down service you need to get this separately. The AA charges around £38 for seven days cover on its Vehicle Plus scheme.

BREAKDOWN ORGANISATION COSTS

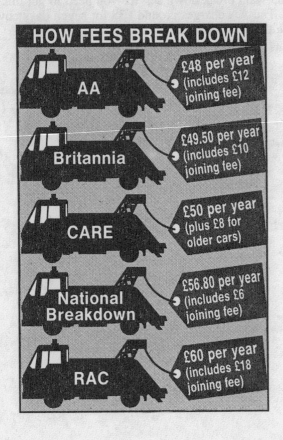

HOW FEES BREAK DOWN

AA — £48 per year (includes £12 joining fee)

Britannia — £49.50 per year (includes £10 joining fee)

CARE — £50 per year (plus £8 for older cars)

National Breakdown — £56.80 per year (includes £6 joining fee)

RAC — £60 per year (includes £18 joining fee)

COSTS OF A CAR LOAN

WHAT IT COSTS FOR A £6,000 CAR LOAN			
Lender	Monthly payment without insurance	Monthly payment with insurance	APR
MIDLAND	£211	£239	17.3%
NAT WEST	£215	£248	18.9%
ABBEY NATIONAL	£217	£243	19.9%
CO-OP	£215	£239	18.94% (uninsured) 17.84% (insured)
LLOYDS	£211	£239	18.1%
HALIFAX	£215	£247	19.2%
NATIONWIDE	£225 (non-customers) £220 (customers)	£251 (non-customers) £244 (customers)	22.9% (non-customers) 20.9% (customers)
TSB	£213	£245	17.9%
BARCLAYS*	£210	£239	17.9%
AA	£206	£254	16.9%

CHAPTER 7

TAX

IT'S just a three-letter word but it gives most people the hee-by-jeebies. Tax! We all have to pay it some time or other. If you work for someone else, you have it deducted from your wages. If you work for yourself, the taxman will work out what you owe him after studying your income and outgoings.

If the thud of the tax demand on the doormat sends shivers down your spine, just tot up all you get in return for your money - roads, schools, hospitals, child benefit, housing, transport, to name just a few. The money has to come from somewhere. And because not enough money goes into the coffers to keep everything ticking over, there's also council tax to keep local services up to scratch, and value added tax (VAT) on some services and goods you buy to add to the national kitty.

Even when you retire, if your income is over a certain level you pay tax on the remainder. But pity the poor taxman. It's not his fault that he has one of the most unpopular jobs in the country. He has to pay tax like the rest of us. But you can oil the wheels and make things a whole lot easier on him and yourself if you get your tax returns in on time.

"Moonlighters" who earn extra cash without letting the tax-man know, then hide the money under the mattress just to dodge paying tax, lose out in the end.

The penalties are severe if they are caught out. Not only that, but they won't be able to invest the money to make the most of it. And the only interest you could get from stowing it away in an old sock, instead of a savings account, is fluff.

The tax you owe is usually simple enough to work out. If you are given a tax code, you'll be able to get a rough idea how much of your money is going to be taxed. The code number shows how much you can earn before you start paying tax. The letter following your number sorts you into a particular group of taxpayers.

For instance, L shows you are under 65 and single; H is for those under 65 claiming the married couple's allowance or the additional personal allowance; P is for anyone single aged 65 to 74; and V is for couples aged 65 to 74 claiming the married couple's allowance.

Those are the four main tax code groups, but there are others which tell an employer what tax you should be paying. If your code is D followed by a number, for example, it means your pay is taxed at the higher rate; NT means no tax is payable on your income.

If you start work without having a tax code, your employer will have to deduct tax under a special emergency code until the taxman has sorted out where you fit in. This could happen if you have not worked before, you've returned from working abroad, or lost your P45.

Under the emergency code, you are only entitled to a single person's allowance, so you could be paying too much tax. If you are entitled to a refund this will be arranged when you get your proper tax code.

Everyone is allowed a certain amount of income before starting to pay tax. That tax-free sum is the personal tax allowance, and it increases with age and when you marry. Remember, it is not a payment to you. It is only the amount of income you can have before you pay income tax, and it can be set against income from a job, savings or pensions.

Above that allowance the next £2,500 you earn is taxed at the lower 20p in the £ rate. From the next tax year- 1994/5- the lower rate band will be increased to £3,000.

Most taxpayers pay basic rate tax of 25p in the £ on the rest of their income.

Higher rate tax of 40p in the £ is charged on anything you earn, after deducting allowances, above £23,701.

Apart from the personal allowance you could be entitled to other allowances which leave you with a larger slice of your income before being taxed.

When you marry, you can decide which of you should get the married couple's allowance, or you can split it between you. Wives have the right to claim half the allowance since April 6, 1993. Basically, it makes sense to transfer the allowance to the person with the most income or the sole breadwinner, to help keep their tax bill down.

Whatever you decide, you need to tell the tax office in the year you marry, and either complete a form or ask the tax office to help you fill it in. There's no need to complete a form every year, but if you say you want to change things again, it won't take effect until the start of the next tax year.

You can claim one twelfth of the married couple's allowance for each tax month of marriage. So the earlier you marry in the tax year, after April 6, the more you increase your tax allowances for that year.

Couples who separate can get the same amount of married couple's allowance they were getting before the separation. If you have a child living with you, you can claim an additional personal allowance as long as you don't get the full married couple's allowance. If you only get half the married couple's allowance you can ask for an additional personal allowance to make it up to the full amount.

Couples don't suddenly lose out when one dies. A woman who gets some of the married couple's allowance in the year her husband dies can claim anything left of her husband's share of the allowance if it's not been used up by his income. She then claims the widow's bereavement allowance.

If the wife dies first, the husband gets all the married couple's allowance less any that his wife used against her income. The following year he will just get his personal allowance unless he remarries.

An additional personal allowance is paid to anyone bringing up a child alone, but a husband can also claim it if his wife is completely disabled.

The child can either be your own or a stepchild, one you adopted before the age of 18, and still in full time education. You can only go on claiming the allowance after the child's sixteenth birthday if they're continuing full-time education or training.

It sometimes happens that you don't get the full additional allowance because your partner is claiming for the child. If that's so, and you are not living with your partner as a married couple but one of you can claim for another child, you should let the tax office know. Both of you may be able to have a full allowance. Or you may decide to give up your claim or share the allowance more evenly.

But if you can't come to an agreement about how to share it out, it will be split according to how much time the child lives with each one.

Unmarried couples living together can only claim one additional allowance between them, for the youngest child.

Anyone registered as blind with a local authority can claim an extra allowance.

You get an extra personal allowance when you reach 65, and it increases again when you're 75, which allows you to keep more of your income from part-time jobs, pensions and savings before you get a tax bill.

If your income goes over a certain level, the age allowance goes down by £1 for every £2 above that threshold until it gets down to the single person's or married couple's allowance. So if your income from savings is pushing you over the limit where you'll have to start paying tax, think about switching into tax-free investments like TESSAs, National Savings Certificates, Personal Equity Plans and Save As You Earn schemes.

An annuity is another way of saving your age allowance from being whittled down. If you buy it with your own cash and not as part of a pension scheme, only part of the income is taxable.

Non-taxpayers, such as children and pensioners, can ask to have interest paid gross on building society or bank savings accounts. Otherwise it is credited to your account with the tax already deducted. If your income is less than your tax allowances you will get the interest paid in full.

The taxman says thousands of pensioners have paid far too much tax because they didn't let anyone know they'd retired and had tax taken off the interest on their savings. If you think yours has been taxed since April 6, 1991, you may be able to claim some or all of it back.

As well as tax allowances, there are other ways of claiming tax relief.

You get relief on the interest paid on a mortgage up to £30,000, or on a loan taken out for home improvement before April 5, 1988. If your lender gives you the tax relief by reducing the interest you pay, under MIRAS (Mortgage Interest Relief at Source), your tax office is not involved. The lender reclaims from Inland Revenue the discount he gave you.

If your loan is not in MIRAS, you pay your lender the full amount of interest and the taxman increases your tax code so you pay less tax. You can only have tax relief on one home at a time, but if you can't sell your old home before you move into the new one, you may be able to get tax relief on both, usually for up to a year.

If you have to pay for a course leading to a national vocational qualification, you should get tax relief at the basic rate for the fees you pay.

And there's tax relief on private medical insurance premiums if you or your partner are over 60, personal pension plans, approved retirement annuity schemes and free-standing additional voluntary contributions schemes to top up your pension benefits.

If you have more than one job you get a separate PAYE code for each one. Your tax bill may need adjusting at the end of the tax year if you think the taxman got your earnings wrong or misunderstood one of your allowances. You can ask him for an assessment to give you an idea of what he thinks you owe.

You'll also get an assessment if you're self-employed. But if you forgot to fill in a tax return, the assessment will be an estimate because the taxman doesn't have enough information about you. You'll know that's what happened if the assessment carries an E in front of the amount you're supposed to have earned.

If you think he's asking too much or got something wrong you have to appeal in writing within 30 days from the date the assessment was issued. You'll also have to ask to postpone payment if you think you're being asked to pay too much.

The taxman will want to know why you think the assessment is wrong, and the amount you want to postpone paying until the matter is settled. When it's all sorted out you'll get a revised assessment.

If your tax bill is too low, don't be tempted to keep quiet about it. The chances are the slip will come to light one day and you'll be charged interest on the difference between what you paid and what you really owed.

Even if you're off work ill, the sick pay you get from the boss is normally taxable. But if it's less than you normally earn each week or month you may be due for a tax refund. It may either be repaid in your normal pay packet, or your tax bill may be altered when you get back to work.

If you lose your job during the tax year, and you claim unemployment benefit, you may get a tax refund at the end of the tax year or when you return to work, whichever happens first.

Your employer should make sure you get a tax refund if you're temporarily laid off work. But workers on strike can't claim a tax refund until they are back at work, unless you leave that job before the strike ends.

If your PAYE code goes up more of your pay is going to be free of tax. It may mean you've been paying too much tax earlier in the year. If your code is only slightly higher you may just have less tax deducted from your wages. If it's gone up quite a bit you should get a tax rebate in your first pay packet with your new tax code.

Your take-home pay will be less if your PAYE goes down. It means you've not been paying enough tax from the start of the tax year, and your employer will have to deduct it. Or you may have forgotten to mention income from letting a room, or from a hobby which earns you extra cash.

If the back tax is a large sum, you may be asked to pay it in one lump plus interest from the date it should have been due. But if you're a pensioner or employee and the amount of tax due is quite small, it can be collected gradually by having your PAYE code lowered. Arrears paid this way would not normally mean having to pay interest charges on top.

You'll know exactly what you earned and how much tax you've paid from the P60 form your employer gives you at the end of the tax year. If you should have claimed additional allowances, or deductions were overlooked which could have lowered your tax bill in the past six years, you should send the details with your P60 to your Inspector of Taxes, asking for a tax refund.

And don't forget that perks can sometimes land you in a mess with the taxman. Inland Revenue rules clamp down on gifts from the boss, like theatre tickets, a Christmas hamper or free hair-dos. They could look like a back-door pay-rise.

An insurance consultant who won a colour television in a raffle at work received a tax demand for £200 months later because the taxman decided it was a "benefit in kind". So it was really a taxable perk, just like having a company car, because it was only something available to employees.

Even gifts made to members of your family may be treated as an indirect gift to you. Special outings or trips for wives, for example, could mean a tax-bill for the hotel and travel costs, unless a husband can prove he had health reasons for needing his wife.

Tax is calculated on the cost of the gift, or how much the employee could sell it for. But modest gifts from a third party, like a bottle of whisky from a grateful client, are not usually taxed.

If you get an award for doing well at your job, that can also be taxable. And bosses who offer cash to long-serving workers on retirement could help them avoid a tax bill by giving them an alternative, such as a gift or shares in the company.

The taxman considers cash as a taxable bonus on top of your normal salary, even when it comes at the end of your working life.

CHAPTER 8

LONG TERM SAVINGS

A PENSION is not the only way of creating a retirement nest egg. There are plenty of other options available - some dull, some exciting.

Basically, it depends on:

- How much risk you're prepared to take.
- Your tax position.
- Whether you want to invest a lump sum or save regularly.
- Whether you need extra income to boost your salary or are investing only for growth.

It is never too soon to start saving. Even a fairly modest amount- say, £50- paid into a building society each month can turn into a sizeable lump sum over the longer term. However, you sacrifice the potentially greater rewards associated with stocks and shares.

Less than 20 per cent of people seek advice on retirement planning. Most stumble into their sixties hoping that their pension, together with some rainy day savings, will maintain their standard of living.

The simple message is: the earlier the better. Even thirtysomething may be too late.

Really, you need a good spread of investments. The golden

rule is: don't put all your eggs in one basket. The options include TESSAs, PERSONAL EQUITY PLANS, UNIT AND INVESTMENT TRUSTS,SHARES AND ENDOWMENT INSURANCE POLICIES.

But only after ensuring you have a "rainy day" emergency fund tucked away in banks, building societies or National Savings, as we explained in Chapter 2.

As retirement looms, it is wise to transfer money from higher risk investments, like shares, into fixed-interest ones that protect your capital and income.

For couples, pre-retirement is also the time to take advantage of independent taxation. If one of you is a higher rate taxpayer consider passing on assets to your partner. The same applies if one of you is a basic rate taxpayer and the other pays no tax. It is best for savings to be in the name of the person paying the lower rate or no tax.

TESSAs.

These are a must for small savers. The investment limit is £9,000 over five years - up to £3,000 in the first year, up to £1,800 in the next three years and £600 in the final year. Interest is paid gross if the account is left untouched for the entire period. If you want to close the account, you just get net interest.

Again, the best TESSA rates are offered by small building societies. Occasionally, fixed rate TESSAs with guaranteed returns are launched. Given the low inflation prospects, these can be attractive. But you may have to invest the entire £9,000 at the outset. This is put into a separate account which drip-feeds the TESSA.

Study the small print and look out for any penalties - for example, if you want to transfer the money to a different bank or building society.

Each adult can open only one Tessa. Non-taxpayers may get higher rates elsewhere.

FRIENDLY SOCIETIES

These offer 10-year tax-free bonds where the maximum

investment allowed by statute is £18 per person a month.

All the above accounts may be risk-free, but there is not much reward either. If you want your savings to grow, there is a compelling reason to at least consider some form of equity investment. According to research by the Household Mortgage Corporation, stocks and shares have been the best-performing investment over the long term. In spite of the 1987 stock market crash, shares have increased by an average of 16.5 per cent a year during the last decade - turning a £1,000 investment made 10 years ago into about £4,500 now.

This beats bricks and mortar, gold and the average building society account, which would have returned just over £2,000. Choosing which shares is the key decision. It's not easy to pick winners. Though individual shares can rise spectacularly, they can sometimes perform disastrously.

"Blue Chip" shares are shares in tip top companies such as BT, Marks and Spencer and Sainsbury, which can be counted on to pay a regular dividend. Charities and other trustee investors are prepared to invest money entrusted with them in these companies. But even Blue Chip shares can disappoint.

UNIT TRUSTS AND INVESTMENT TRUSTS

Perhaps the best way into the stock market is through these "collective" funds. Unit trusts pool money to buy a range of shares. Professional fund managers take the decisions for you, and the risk is spread because they buy a small share in lots of investments.

Traditionally, unit trusts have divided into "income" and "growth" funds. But there are now many specialist funds investing in, say, smaller companies, industrial sectors and overseas markets. If you pick the right fund, you can beat the average uplift in the UK stockmarket.

A good place to start is with a general UK equity fund. These invest in a broad range of UK shares. Or you could try a "tracker" fund, designed to give a similar rate of growth to the stockmarket.

You can invest in a unit trust directly or through a stockbroker or financial adviser. It is important to opt for a good fund manager. Study their track record rather than any projections they make. Sticking with one of the well-known groups is wise. Avoid the trap of picking the best fund of the previous year - the chances are it will soon run out of steam.

Also check out the charges, which can be high. Normally there is an up-front charge of five per cent, with annual management fees typically 1.5 per cent. Annual fees for investment trusts are lower - usually between 0.25 and one per cent.

Investment trusts, which have been around since the 1860s, are companies that invest in the shares of other companies. This means you can buy one share yet invest in perhaps 100 companies.

Like unit trusts, you can opt for general or specialist investment trusts. Over the longer term, investment trusts tend to perform better than unit trusts. According to Micropal, £100 a month put in the best-performing investment trust over the last five years is today worth more than £10,000. This is a creditable performance for what should be considered the shortest period for equity investment.

Many trusts operate regular savings schemes starting from as little as £40 a month. The risk is less than it is for lump sum investors, who are vulnerable to sudden stockmarket falls.

In fact, monthly savers can benefit from stockmarket volatility through a process called "pound cost averaging": when prices are low, your regular payment buys more than when prices are high. But the long-term trend must be upward for you to profit.

The objective of most savings schemes is long-term capital growth.

All you do is arrange a direct debit from your bank account. The trust then buys as many shares as can be afforded each month. Apart from convenience, savings scheme charges are lower than going through a broker.

If you do decide to invest in equities, go for one wrapped in a personal equity plan, otherwise you are liable for income tax and capital gains tax.

PERSONAL EQUITY PLANS

You can invest up to £6,000 a year in a general Pep, plus another £3,000 in a single company Pep. Returns are exempt from income tax and capital gains tax. And you can cash-in without penalty at any time.

Basically, there are three different types of Pep: "managed" (where a company chooses the stocks for you), "self select" (where you choose the stocks yourself) and those run by unit and investment trusts.

Only buy a Pep if you want to invest in the stockmarket anyway, not because of the tax breaks. Some Peps have high charges, which could wipe out the tax advantages.

According to investment advisers Chase de Vere, there are more than 100 Pep savings schemes.

INFLATION

This is the big enemy of savers, and it is dangerous to assume it has been licked for ever. For example, an annual rate of four per cent, the top of the Government's target range, over 10 years, reduces the purchasing power of £1,000 to less than £700.

Index-linked National Savings certificates are the traditional hedge against inflation. These can be bought from post offices. They normally offer a bonus above inflation, and the maximum investment is £10,000.

Index-linked gilts are an alternative. These Government Securities get the name of gilts or gilt-edged securities because the Government guarantees that you'll get your money back. The Bank of England has published a guide for small investors, available free by ringing 0800 616814. National Savings offer an array of account and bonds. Maturing certificates can usually be reinvested in new issues, so it is possible to build up a hefty retirement lump sum.

With-profits endowment policies, where annual bonuses are added to a final maturity value can provide respectable returns. They have been criticised for being inflexible and expensive because of the high commission taken by salesmen. The key point is to choose a life insurance company with a good track record.

PENSIONS

Your pension is likely to be your most important retirement asset. Unfortunately most people are not well provided for. If you have changed jobs several times, taken a break to bring up children or worked in non-pensionable employment you will probably end up retiring with less (sometimes much less) than the maximum - two-thirds of your final salary.

Additional Voluntary Contributions (AVCs) are a simple solution to the shortfall in retirement funds.

Most employees pay only about five per cent of their income into an employer's scheme, though they can commit up to 15 per cent of their gross earnings and still get tax relief.

You have an absolute right to contribute to an outside AVC fund, and there are a wide range of Free-standing AVCs (FSAVCs) available from insurance companies.

But there is a price to pay for the tax relief. Unlike your main pension, you cannot commute all or part of your AVCs into a lump sum when you retire. The amount that you build up is used to provide an income, which is then taxable.

Some people prefer the flexibility of a Pep, where income from investments is tax-free and you can take all the capital when you like. But there is no tax relief on the money you put into a Pep.

In general, it is a mistake to switch from a decent employer's scheme to a personal pension, though commission-hungry salesmen may try to persuade you otherwise.

HOW THE CASH GROWS

	JAN 1 1983	JAN 1 1988	JAN 1 1993
Halifax BS 90-day notice	£1,000	£1,530	£2,256
NatWest Bank Instant Access	£1,000	£1,540	£2,490
FTSE 100 shares	£1,000	£2,610	£4,420
Investment Trust	£1,000	£2,464	£5,563
Unit Trust	£1,000	£1,421	£4,903
Gilts	£1,000	£1,085	£1,239
National Savings Certificates	£1,000	£1,470	£2,363
Pension Plan (basic rate taxpayer)	£1,000	£2,387	£7,138
Pension Plan (higher rate taxpayer)	£1,000	£2,983	£12,489
House	£1,000	£1,700	£1,950
Investment Bond	£1,000	£1,923	£3,232
Gold	£1,000	£875.11	£762.69
Stamps	£1,000	£1,095	£1,308

Sources: Halifax Building Society, NatWest Bank, ProShare, Association of Investment Trusts, Unit Trust Association of Unit Trusts and Investment Funds, National Savings, Building Societies Association, Standard Life Assurance, Gold Fields Minerals Services, Sotherbys, Stanley Gibbons.

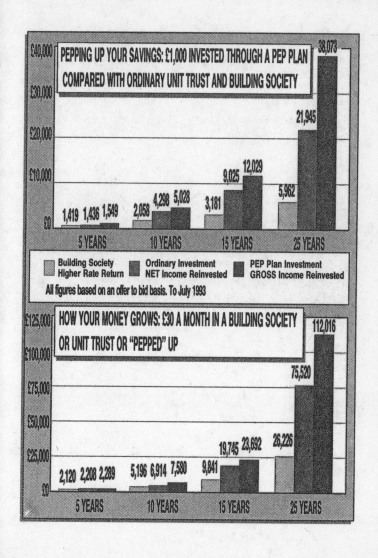

PEPPING UP YOUR SAVINGS: £1,000 INVESTED THROUGH A PEP PLAN COMPARED WITH ORDINARY UNIT TRUST AND BUILDING SOCIETY

5 YEARS: 1,419 / 1,436 / 1,549
10 YEARS: 2,058 / 4,298 / 5,028
15 YEARS: 3,181 / 9,025 / 12,029
25 YEARS: 5,962 / 21,945 / 38,073

☐ Building Society Higher Rate Return
■ Ordinary Investment NET Income Reinvested
■ PEP Plan Investment GROSS Income Reinvested

All figures based on an offer to bid basis. To July 1993

HOW YOUR MONEY GROWS: £30 A MONTH IN A BUILDING SOCIETY OR UNIT TRUST OR "PEPPED" UP

5 YEARS: 2,120 / 2,208 / 2,289
10 YEARS: 5,196 / 6,914 / 7,580
15 YEARS: 9,841 / 19,745 / 23,692
25 YEARS: 26,226 / 75,520 / 112,016

101

H.G.H. - 6

CHAPTER 9

REDUNDANCY

BEING made redundant is now a fact of life for most working people and is likely to remain so into the next century. Jobs for life are virtually non-existent, with most people having to change jobs at least twice and possibly even more frequently during their working lifetime.

With job loss comes debt almost as inevitably as night follows day, but it is possible to survive by managing your debt intelligently. Debt market analysts, Mintel, say there are some 1,800,000 households in Britain owing a total of £2 billion to 3,300,000 creditors. So you're by no means alone if you're in debt!

But there's a difference between those in debt and those in deep financial trouble: And the difference comes down to how effectively you can manage the problem.

Managing debt must start immediately you lose your job. Taking firm control of your total financial resources must be your first priority after being made redundant. Next most important is the remedy - getting another job.

If you have been given some sort of notice then count your blessings. Whilst you are still in your old job there are several steps you can take to ease the pain and limit your debt.

If your present boss provides any sort of free life or medical insurance, make sure you ask if the firm will extend the cover for a period after you leave them. They might even allow you to renew medical insurance without further medical checks. For those with dependents it is essential that you try and keep this cover.

It is essential to draw up a list of all your payouts to everyone - gas, electricity, hire purchase, overdraft, mortgage or rent payments - the lot. Now you must do some severe financial pruning. Cut out everything that is not essential: Subscriptions to social clubs, magazines, even hire purchase debt.

If you have direct debits and standing orders review the lot! Are they necessary? If you are lucky enough to have some redundancy cash coming to you use it to pay off your credit card debt or overdraft. Don't use it to pay off part of your mortgage - at least not yet.

Your mortgage will almost certainly be your single biggest headache - and avoiding being repossessed should have top priority.

Repossession is relatively easy to avoid if you act early and deal openly with the building society, bank or other mortgage lender.

The key point for anyone unable to meet the mortgage is not to suffer in silence. Share the problem with the local building society manager as soon as possible. Don't wait for one moment after you've been made redundant. Contact the manager and tell the people who have lent you money what the problem is.

Believe it or not building societies hate repossessing homes. In these days of falling house prices they are actually likely to lose money if they have to 'distress' sell your home. Building societies in particular believe it is far better to try and ease you through the period of indebtedness.

To this end they will suggest a series of alternatives to enable you to continue living in your home.

If you have a REPAYMENT mortgage it may be possible to reduce your monthly payments by extending the mortgage from say 25 to 30 years, for example. Or the lender might be prepared to accept interest only payments until you are back on your feet.

It will be easier for them to do this if your home is worth more than you originally paid for it.

Unfortunately many homeowners are now living in homes where they have 'negative equity'. In other words their home is worth less than they paid for it because of falling property prices.

Even with these drawbacks the building societies will try to come to some sort of a financial arrangement to allow you to continue living in the home of your choice.

For those with ENDOWMENT mortgages it might be possible to persuade the society manager to lower the interest rate charged for a while. Another alternative might be to persuade the building society to switch your mortgage from an Endowment to a Repayment mortgage.

On both Repayment and Endowment mortgages some building societies have allowed homeowners to add their outstanding arrears on to the sum owed and for it to be paid off when better times return.

You may well qualify for help with your mortgage interest from Social Security. Indeed, your mortgage lender may insist that you put in a claim even if you are not sure you qualify. For it is in his interest as much as yours to prevent you falling into arrears.

Some building societies operate mortgage-to-rent schemes though these are few and far between. Lenders allow homebuyers to who can't repay their mortgages to revert to being tenants, paying rent only until their circumstances improve. Latest statistics show that just 300 home owners have been saved from eviction by such schemes. The advantage of becoming a tenant in this way is that the former homebuyer with a mortgage then qualifies for further state benefits.

Those who rent homes must also take swift action. It does not matter who you pay rent to - local Council, housing association or private landlord - the most important step is to contact the local Department of Social Security Office, Housing Aid Centre (if there is one in your area) or Local Authority (Council).

Housing benefit is obtainable from these bodies, but be patient as the bureaucracy takes a long time! Once again ensure that you have details of your income and the rent you pay and to whom, with plenty of documentary proof.

As soon as you have been made jobless you must sign on for your State benefits.

Too many redundant people shy away from this because of the stigma that has been built up by politicians against 'scroungers'. Remember you have paid for these benefits over the years with huge tax and National Insurance payments. So don't be put off.

Even if you are not entitled to benefit signing on ensures that at the very least your National Insurance contributions will be paid. That will secure your state pension when you reach retirement age.

And if you have a mortgage you should contact Social Security right away to see whether you qualify for help meeting your mortgage interest.

If you have been laid off part way through the tax year (April to March) don't forget to apply for a rebate from the taxman. If you can convince them that you are suffering financial hardship you can get paid early. Obtain Form IR 41 called Income Tax and the Unemployed for detailed advice.

If you have received a lump sum pay-off for goodness sake don't squander it. The simplest and safest way of looking after your money is to put it into a building society or bank.

Don't tie it up for long periods. Get an account that will enable you to draw money when you want to and earn interest.

The interest you get may be a little less but at least the money is safe and sound and available for all emergencies.

And if you are no longer liable to income tax fill in the necessary form to get the interest paid to you gross - without tax being deducted.

The worst aspect of being unemployed is the instant lack of routine on Day One of Unemployment. Try and get into a scheduled day that involves family and friends. Go to the support services provided by the state in Jobcentres and by local authorities.

Jobcentres have New Client Advisers who will give advice about benefits. But before seeing them you must start to get on top of your own financial affairs. Details of your existing income before being made redundant are most important. Rent or mortgage repayment details will be needed with documentary proof. All the documents you have on Council Tax, your personal savings, the income and savings of your personal dependents (spouse and/or children) and anyone who lives in the same household. Before you go to the benefits offices leaflets FB9, NI 12, IS 1 and IS 20 provide details of unemployment benefits and income support.

Local Council services for the unemployed vary dramatically, but contact your City Hall or District Council offices. There is not much cash available but there are concessions for the unemployed even if only for travel and sports activities. Get them as part of the process of shifting into a new routine that has been lost through being jobless.

Don't forget that if your savings are less than £16,000 you will be entitled to Council Tax benefit. This will be paid on a sliding scale according to the savings you have.

For those on low income with one or more dependents under 16 years of age with savings of less than £8,000. there are family credit benefits available. Again they are paid on a sliding scale according to the savings.

Income support is also available for those with savings below £8,000.

If you find yourself trapped in debt seek advice. Surprisingly only one in seven of those seriously in debt ask for advice.

Yet it is available. The Citizens Advice Bureaux are enormously experienced and practical about dealing with individual debt - after all, everyone's problem is different.

And if they cannot help they can put you in touch with a specialist advice centre.

They can often help negotiate with your creditors and help you come to some arrangement.

But it is essential that you offer to make some attempt to repay at least some of what you owe - no matter how small - and stick to it.

No creditor is stupid enough to ignore the person who is attempting to repay debt - even if the amount is very small.

But one of the conditions of schemes like this is that you cannot attempt to get further into debt. If you are hopelessly in debt it is still worth while trying to remedy the situation. Dun and Bradstreet, the world's largest suppliers of business information on firms - they can provide financial details on 2.2 million British businesses and some 22 million worldwide - reckon it costs British companies £8,000 in time and resources for every £1000 lost to debt.

Dun and Bradstreet are just one of many agencies who specialise in keeping information on bad debtors. They all make charges to creditors wanting to find out information about the credit rating of a firm or individual.

For the ordinary person in debt the first inkling of trouble is when you receive a notice taking you to court for failing to pay a debt. This is a County Court summons or Small Claims Court summons.

The first step is to draw up details of what you are earning (your incomings - even if it is only state benefits) and what you are spending (outgoings). Go down with this to the Citizens Advice Bureau and tell them your problem. They do have debt counsellors who are extremely experienced.

You must always turn up at the County Court hearing otherwise the judgment will almost automatically go against you. Armed with your details of earnings and outgoings tell the court judge exactly how much you can afford to pay off. If possible keep paying at least some of the money you owe in the run up to the County Court appearance.

Generally judges are sympathetic to those who try to manage debts especially if they appear in court to explain their problem.

Sometimes Small Claims Courts sit in judgment on debts. Basically the procedure is just the same - except there is more informality to make individuals feel at ease. They involve sums of less than £1000 (£250 in Scotland).

Before you go to any of these courts it is a good idea to pop along before your hearing to listen to what goes on and see the procedures. It also familiarises you with the surroundings, legal language and the way the court and judges go about their work.

Generally these Courts are concerned to get some sort of payment from the person in debt - no matter how insignificant.

The big disadvantage of receiving a County Court or Small Claims Court summons is that it is one of the many statistics that are collected by credit information service companies. In 1992 there were 430,000 County Court judgments in England alone - a record. It is even worse if a Court order is made against you as this goes on the records and makes it very difficult for you to obtain credit in the future.

If you discover that you are recorded as being a bad debtor you do have the right to see the information (on payment of a small fee) to note if it is correct. Sometimes credit agencies have made awful mistakes and you do have the right to tell them the information they possess is incorrect.

Useful telephone number:- National Debtline - 021-368 8501.

Citizens Advice Bureau - look in your local phonebook for the address and telephone number.

Is it possible to protect yourself from falling into debt? In particular is it possible to protect against the biggest financial fear for the person owning their home - losing earnings to cover that monthly mortgage repayment?

Redundancy insurance, or 'mortgage payment protection' will provide cover if you are unable to work because you have been made redundant, become disabled or even if you are fired. Even the self-employed can take out redundancy insurance to protect themselves if their business goes bust.

The policy usually pays out a set amount, typically around £1000 or one-and-a-quarter times your mortgage repayment-whichever is lower. The policy payout is usually after you have been out of work for one or two months and is therefore paid in arrears.

These days some building societies insist on selling redundancy insurance with their mortgage, though this is not always so. There are schemes available at any time in the life of a mortgage. But like all insurance policies READ THE SMALL PRINT.

Many policies don't cover those who opt for voluntary

redundancy. Working less than 16 hours a week or even on fixed term contracts, can incur penalties. There are also drawbacks in the small print for those becoming unemployed for the second time within six months of the last claim, pregnancy related illnesses and disabilities that make you unable to work.

Perhaps the major disadvantage of redundancy insurance to cover a mortgage is that it affects state benefits for those who become unemployed. In particular it could lead to a loss of benefit for those with mortgages whereby the state pays the interest element of their mortgage whilst they are unemployed.

Always remember when buying redundancy insurance to read the small print before you make up your mind and sign on the dotted line.

CHAPTER 10

COMPLAINTS

HOW safe is your money? It's a big, bad world out there and it's filled with conmen trying to get their hands on your hard-earned cash.

Many of us will invest our money with well-known firms thinking they'll give us extra protection.

Most of the time that's the case. But you don't have to invest with conman outfits a like Barlow Clowes to put your money at risk. The smooth-talking salesman lurks round every corner, eager to clinch a deal that's going to leave HIM quids in.

Even if you've got your money in a savings account at a reputable bank or in a policy with a well-known investment firm it's never 100 per cent safe.

Mistakes can happen, for starters – and far more often than you realise. So what can you do if your money goes astray, or a salesman gives you duff advice?

BANKS AND BUILDING SOCIETIES

The big banks may seem fearsome institutions but they're certainly not above the law. And just as well.

According to the latest Which? magazine survey a growing number of Britain's bank and building society customers reckon they've been on the receiving end of shoddy treatment. It revealed that ONE in FIVE customers had a problem with a direct debit or standing order.

One in seven had money wrongly taken out of their account and one in ten had been wrongly charged.

If this happens to you, your first problem will be spotting the mistake. So ALWAYS check your statements carefully.

But once you've spotted a mistake your problems aren't necessarily over.

Putting it right can be a frustrating and time consuming process so it's important to do things by the book:

● Never lose your temper – that can be counter-productive.

● Many problems can be put right with a simple phone call but make sure you get the full name of the person you're speaking to.

● If that gets you nowhere put your complaint IN WRITING stating what you want them to do and when you want it done by. You can also claim compensation for the time you've spent sorting out the problem. Claim for the cost of your phone calls, for instance. And try claiming for each letter you send out. Many banks and building societies charge between £10 to £15 for a letter they send YOU so give them a taste of their own medicine and charge them the same rate for your letters.

● Keep copies of all your correspondence with the bank and make sure any assurances made to you, on the phone or in person, are put in writing.

● If you're not happy with your branch's response write to the head office. If that gets you nowhere write to the Banking Ombudsman at 70 Gray's Inn Road, London WC1X 8NB (071-404-9944) or the Building Societies Ombudsman, Grosvenor Gardens House, 35-37 Grosvenor Gardens, London SW1X 7AW (071 931 0044).

THE OMBUDSMAN

The Ombudsman can only deal with complaints that have reached "deadlock" – where the bank or building society has made its final ruling.

If your complaint hasn't reached this stage it will be referred back to your bank and building society.

The Ombudsman has limited powers. For instance, he can't make a ruling:

● About your credit worthiness.

● Where legal action is taking place.

● Where you are not personally affected.

And if you've got a general gripe, about the size of overdraft charges, for example, there's nothing he can do about that.

But he can make rulings on disputed transactions, mortgage payments and bad advice.

And he can ensure the banks and building societies abide by the Code of Practice. And if they don't he can award compensation of up to £100,000.

Areas the Code covers include:

● The publishing of charges and changes in interest rates. One of the most common gripes for savers is the way some building societies lure them in with bumper interest rates only to lower them soon afterwards. If the Ombudsman decides a drop in a savings rate hasn't been publicised enough he can award the customer compensation for the loss of interest.

● The limiting of liability where a card had been lost or stolen. Under the Code a customer cannot be liable for any more than £50 of any unauthorised withdrawal unless the bank or building society can prove fraud or gross negligence.

INVESTMENTS

The good news is there are laws to protect you from the slick salesman and investment shark. The 1986 Finance Services Act set up watchdogs to protect the ordinary investor.

By law all investment firms now have to belong to one of these watchdogs. These are called "authorised" firms.

If you invest with a firm which isn't authorised you're on very dangerous ground. If your money goes missing you have virtually no come-back.

You can check the firm is authorised by phoning the SIB

on 071 929 3652. Before you go to the regulator you should first complain IN WRITING to the company.

Put your evidence together carefully. Jot down the main points you wish to raise. Make notes of the dates of any letters or phone calls between you and the firm. It helps if you can remember the names of the people you have spoken to.

Keep your letter as clear as possible and only make points which are RELEVANT. If your letter is too long or rambling it might slow up the complaint. A typed letter always helps.

Include copies of relevant documents – NEVER send originals.

If your firm fails to reply or if you're unhappy about their response you can take your complaint to the regulator. They will investigate your complaint independently.

The regulator's name should appear on the firm's notepaper. If it's not there you can get the name from the SIB.

Who you write to also depends on the type of complaint.

Complaints about shady sales practices are handled by LAUTRO or FIMBRA.

LAUTRO – the Life Assurance and Unit Trust Regulatory Association – is the watchdog body that supervises life insurance and unit trust companies.

FIMBRA – Financial Intermediaries, Managers and Brokers Regulatory Association – is the watchdog for salesmen, brokers and independent advisers.

LAUTRO'S rules cover people who have bought a policy from a firm's representative or from an appointed representative or 'tied agent'. The 'tied agent' will work for a company with a different name but represent the company or society.

LAUTRO's address is Centre Point, 103 New Oxford Street, London WC1A 1QH (071 379 0444)

If you bought a policy through an Independent Financial Adviser – or IFA – you can complain to FIMBRA at Hertsmere House, Hertsmere Road, London E14 4AB (071 538 8860).

Both their rules cover:

● Misleading adverts or brochures.

● Salesmen who give you incorrect information or pester you or who sell you the wrong investment or an unsuitable one.

● Salesmen who pretend to offer independent advice.

● Salesmen who persuade you, against your interests, to cash in one product and buy another one – this is called "churning".

But remember their rules only cover the selling and marketing of investments. Here's what ISN'T covered:

● Administrative problems – if the firm fails to collect a direct debit for instance.

● Investments bought before 29 April 1988.

● Products which are not investments, such as loans and mortgages, although endowments or pensions linked to such products are covered by LAUTRO rules.

Complaints about the administration of a unit trust or a pension should go to IMRO at Broadwalk House, 5 Appold Street, London EC2A 2AA (071 628 6022). IMRO – the Investment Management Regulatory Authority – is the watchdog for the people who actually invest and manage savers' money.

If you bought a policy from an accountant write to The Institute of Chartered Accountants in England and Wales, Moorgate Place, London EC2P 2BJ (071 920 8100).

Or if it was from a solicitor write to The Law Society, 113 Chancery lane, London WC2A 1PL (071 242 1222).

The regulators have the power to fine companies who have broken the rules. They can also suggest a figure for compensation, although they can't force the firm to pay up.

If that happens you'll have to take your complaint to:

● The Insurance Ombudsman, 31 Southampton Row, London WC1B 5HJ who deals with life assurance and unit trusts.

● The Investment Ombudsman, 6 Fredrick Place, London EC2R 8BT, who covers pension funds and investments by banks.

If they believe your complaint is justified they can order the company:

● to cover your financial loss.

● to put you back in the position you were in before the cause of the complaint took place. That means working out what your money COULD have earned elsewhere.

The Ombudsman can also compensate for any distress that has been caused.

THE INVESTORS COMPENSATION SCHEME

If a firm goes to the wall or gets into difficulty the Investors Compensation Scheme can declare it to be in default. That means the firm is unable to pay its investors. If that happens you have to make a claim within six months.

But remember the Scheme can only help you if the firm was "authorised." The maximum compensation you can get is £48,000. The first £30,000 of a claim will be met in full and 90 per cent of the next £20,000. So a person who lost £50,000, for instance, would receive £48,000.

The amount you are paid reflects the value of your investment on the date the firm goes bust. So if the firm promised you a "guaranteed" 15 per cent interest a year, for instance, you'll only get back what the Scheme believes to be a realistic figure based on how similar policies have performed.

SPOTTING THE COWBOYS

Prevention is always better than cure, of course. So you'll need to know how to spot the investment cowboys:

Here are the questions to ask BEFORE you talk about investments:

● Is your financial advisor AUTHORISED?

● What kind of investments is the firm authorised to advise upon? Some firms are only allowed to advise on life assurance and unit trusts, for example.

● Is the firm authorised to hold your money? If it's not then only make your cheques out to the firm you're investing with. For example, if the salesman recommends a particular unit trust make your cheque out to the unit trust management. NEVER make a cheque out to an individual no matter how honest he seems.

Your next step is to look for certain tell-tale signs. This very often comes down to your instincts but be wary:

● If the salesman offers you a rate of return higher than anyone else. If the rewards seem too good to be true they probably are. And remember that a "guaranteed" return is only as good as the person who makes the guarantee.

● If he offers you the chance to invest in a "special" scheme which you've never heard of and he can't explain in detail.

● If he fails to ask you about your financial commitments and other investments. If he doesn't have that information he's not going to be able to give you the right advice about the type of investment you need.

● If he advises you to cash in some or all of your existing investments and give the money to him to invest. This is called "churning" and is a serious offence.

● If the salesman has a particularly lavish lifestyle.

● If he advises you to put all your money into one particular investment.

● If he comes across as too pushy or claims there is a pressing reason why you have to invest immediately.

And don't be taken in by someone who seems extremely nice or who has gone to a lot of trouble. Remember it's YOUR money, so don't put yourself into a position where you feel you don't want to say "no" to him.

KEEPING TABS ON YOUR MONEY

They say there's no rest for the wicked but the blameless have their work cut out, too.

For once you have parted with your money you're going to have to keep an eye on it. That means:

● Keeping records of your investment. When you take out an investment it's VITAL you get a RECEIPT. You'll need this if you have to make a claim against the firm or if it goes bust and you claim compensation. So make sure you look after it. And make sure the receipt is from the right people. If you've made your cheque out to a life assurance firm through a broker, for instance, the receipt should be signed by that life assurance firm.

● Checking that you're going to receive regular reports about your investment.

Reports should come every year and should be in writing. A phone call telling you everything is okay is not good enough. Hang on to the reports. They will be useful if you ever have to make a claim for compensation.

WARNING SIGNS

With over 40,000 investment businesses in Britain it's hardly surprising the regulators can't keep their eyes on all of them.

So it's very often down to the investor to spot the tell-tale signs of a firm in trouble.

The warning bells should start ringing:

● If you don't hear anything about your investment within a year.

● If your investments do very well in the middle of a slump. It could be the firm is paying unrealistically high rates using new investors' cash. If that is happening the firm is heading for a crash.

● If you wish to withdraw part of your investment but your advisor makes excuses.

● If you suspect your firm is less than honest tell the regulator straight away.

● It can launch an investigation and tackle the problem before it gets out of hand.

Who knows, your vigilance might just put the mockers on the next Barlow Clowes.

For further information phone the SIB on 071 638 1240 and order a copy of their free leaflets, How to Spot the Investment Cowboys, Compensation for Investors, and What to do if you Need to Complain.

For more information about the Ombudsmen, write to their offices and ask for a copy of their annual report.

CHAPTER 11

DIVORCE

A MAN of 86 got married recently – for the 28th time. His wife was less experienced – this was only her 14th wedding. He said he hasn't given up hope of finding the right woman, but he has made a lot of mistakes so far. You probably guessed it - the ceremony took place in America. In this country we are a bit more cautious about tying the knot.

Even so, more people are getting divorced than ever before. Nearly half today's marriages will end in divorce and it is creating a lot of problems, both emotional and financial.

Marriages don't break down overnight. It takes months or years for a couple to come to the point of admitting that they can no longer live together. Even so you are never prepared for it. Very often people get bitter when they divorce, particularly if one partner has gone off with somebody else. This is a very unpleasant time but you'll come out of it much better if you keep calm and co-operate in sorting out the mess.

Your emotions are on a roller-coaster. You'll feel depressed and frightened of the future. You'll worry yourself sick about the children. This is quite usual. Everyone getting divorced goes through it and you will, in time, get better. It might take a couple of years before you feel normal again but you'll get there eventually.

You'll recover more quickly if you come out of the relationship feeling that you have been treated fairly. Your instincts are to fight for your own survival. You want to get your hands on every penny you can. This is not the way to reach a happy ending. On the other hand, if you agree to whatever your partner suggests because you want to get the whole thing over and done with, you'll regret it. You'll talk to friends afterwards and they'll say you've been a fool.

Then you'll get angry but it may be too late to change your mind. You must accept that you'll both be worse off financially after the divorce. There is no way round it. There is not suddenly going to be any more money but now there are two households to support.

Young couples with good jobs but no children suffer the least. But even they have a lower standard of living because they're no longer sharing their resources. This is often a time when debt problems start. With all the upheavals going on in your life, paying the bills can be the last straw. But if you don't, you'll sink into serious debt which only complicates your problems.

THE PROCEDURE

In fact the actual process of getting divorced is quite simple. It is all the haggling about who owns what that makes it messy. As long as you agree how to divide your possessions, including what happens to your home and who keeps the cat, you can do it by yourselves without using a solicitor. The Citizens Advice Bureau can help you fill out the forms.

It is better to avoid solicitors if you can. For one thing it saves money. The more you pay a solicitor, the less you have for yourself.

Once lawyers are involved, the whole process takes longer and gets nastier. Each solicitor fights for his or her own client. Immediately you are forced into confrontation. In fact, some lawyers are so worried about this that they have set up a group called the Solicitors Family Law Association. Lawyers who belong aim to handle divorce cases as pleasantly as possible. The Law Society in London can put you in touch with them.

HOW IT WORKS

If you want a DIY divorce, you first contact the Principal

Registry in London or your local divorce county court. This is listed in the telephone directory under Courts.In Scotland, divorce is dealt with by the sheriff courts. You must have been married for at least one year. In Scotland you don't have to wait that long. You send them a form, called a 'petition'.This costs £40 but the price can change in future. If you get income support, family credit or legal aid you won't have to pay.

You will be asked the reason for the breakdown of your marriage, that is your grounds for wanting a divorce. This is not the place to start listing all your partner's faults. There are five reasons which the court will accept:

● Your husband or wife has committed adultery.

● Their behaviour is so bad you can't live with them any longer.

● They deserted you at least two years ago.

● You have lived apart for two years and both agree to the divorce

● You have lived apart for five years.

If the court agrees it will say that your marriage has irretrievably broken down.

In time, you get a decree nisi, which is a provisional decree. Then six weeks' later you can apply for the decree absolute. This costs £15. In Scotland there is a single decree which takes effect immediately. At any stage you can change your minds and call the whole thing off. All you need do is tell the court you want to stay married and they will very happily forget all about it. As part of filling in the divorce papers, you need to show how you are dividing up your possessions. Try to do this as amicably as you can and co-operate as much as possible. That means you'll get the whole process settled sooner and you can get on with the rest of your life.

To start with, both of you should write several lists. One with everything you think is your own personal property such as gifts from your parents and to each other. Then write down what you think you own jointly. The house, the car, furniture, kitchen equipment, books, tapes and CDs, the television and video, cameras and radios. Walk round the house with a sheet of paper and note down everything you can find. Add to this list all your financial assets such as life insurance policies. You need to get a cash-in value from the insurance company and the one whose name is on the policy should make a money compensation to the other. Your savings might be personal property or they may be joint possessions. Then sit down together, see how your lists compare and try to come to agreement about who keeps what. If necessary, put a price on the assets you want to keep so you can compensate your partner with money instead. Now you need a budget. Write down how much money you'll have coming in from your own earnings after the divorce. And how much you'll have to pay out.

Find out how much your spouse is earning and how much money he or she has tucked away that you're not meant to know about. You have to balance what you need to live on with how much your ex can afford to pay. For divorcing couples who have no children, judges prefer the clean break. So, if the judge decides you are entitled to money, it means taking a lump sum of cash rather than regular payments. Typically, the wife takes the house instead of receiving maintenance. If you've got a job and no children, you might not get anything. You don't have to be divorced to claim maintenance payments through the court but you must be permanently separated.

THE CHILDREN

You can divorce the person you married but you can never stop being a parent. A divorce that involves children is even more upsetting. The welfare and happiness of your children must come first. This is what the law demands. The court will want to be sure you have made proper arrangements for your children. You must decide where they'll live, where they'll go to school, the access times for the other parent and financial support. If you are asking for regular payments, you now need to go through the government's Child Support Agency.

The Child Support Agency started in April 1993. Partly this is to track down runaway fathers who refuse to pay up for their children. But it also decides the level of child maintenance payments when parents divorce. In fact it can apply to people who already have an agreed settlement, even when this was a clean break agreement. It is going to make quite a difference to divorce arrangements once the system has settled down.

The Child Support Agency sets down a standard formula for working out how much maintenance fathers must pay for their youngsters when they split. Or how much mothers must pay if it works out that way. You have to pay a fee for this unless you receive benefits. The formula includes the day-to-day cost of looking after a child and an element for the mother's expenses. At any time in future she can go back to the Agency for a new assessment. The one who looks after the kids most of the time is called the 'parent with care'. The other one is the 'absent parent'.The Child Poverty Action Group has helpful leaflets explaining what happens. The CPAG is at 4th floor, 1-5 Bath Street, London EC1V 9PY. Telephone: 071-2533406.

TAX RELIEF ON MAINTENANCE PAYMENTS

You can pay as much maintenance as you want, or as the court decides, but you get tax relief only up to a certain limit. This is the same figure as the married couple's allowance. There is no tax relief on any higher payments. If you are paying to more than one ex-wife, you are still only get tax relief on the same upper limit.

You have to pay the money gross to your ex-spouse, which means sending the full amount including tax. You then get tax relief through your PAYE coding if you are employed or through your tax bill.

The person receiving maintenance does not have to pay tax on the money she gets although she has to write it down on her tax return. You should work out carefully how much social security benefits you are entitled to. It might be that the maintenance payments push you just over the limit for income support. Over a certain figure you lose £1 of income support for each £1 of child support. As income support opens the doors to free prescriptions and milk, you could be better off accepting lower maintenance. If you make voluntary maintenance payments, these cannot been forced by law but you won't get any tax relief. Nor do you get tax relief if you make the payments direct to the children and it counts as the kids' own income. Immediately your ex-spouse remarries, your tax relief stops.

But if you remarry you must keep up the payments and you'll still get tax relief (unless you remarry the person you just divorced). Make sure your ex takes out life insurance. When he dies, your maintenance comes to an end. And you might have no pension either. An insurance policy will pay you a lump sum to give you at least some money to live on.The insurance policy should be written 'in trust' for you, then you are certain that you, and nobody else, gets the money. Old rules still apply to tax on maintenance agreements dating before March 1988.

TAX

The Inland Revenue needs to know what is going on. You can't claim the married couple's tax allowance once you stop living together. This won't apply if you have a trial separation or if you are living apart temporarily because one of you is working abroad or in prison. But it will if you are living apart permanently, or you have signed a separation agreement. And obviously if you are divorced. Then you only get the personal tax allowance.

In some circumstances the taxman might say you are living apart even if you are still living under the same roof. This could happen if you have divided the house in two so you each have your own living space including your own kitchen.

If you have at least one child living with you, you can claim the additional personal allowance. The definition of a child is a youngster under the age of 16 or one still in full-time education. This can be your own child, a step-child or one you have legally adopted. The more allowances you claim, the less tax you have to pay. In any case you don't have to pay tax on family credit, housing benefit, income support unless you get it through unemployment or being on strike. Nor do you pay tax on maternity allowance and maternity payment, and any money given to you voluntarily by relatives.

MONEY

There are dozens of details to think about when you get divorced. They seem irrelevant at the time when you are just worrying about surviving day by day. But they are important. And you should tackle the matter at an early stage. If you have a joint bank account or joint savings accounts you should split them right now. Write to the bank or building society and explain what is going on. Say you want to close the joint account and open a new account in your name only. Tell your partner what you are doing. If you suspect that your partner might take all the money out of your joint accounts, phone the bank and arrange for cheques to need both your signatures to be valid. Then you can still draw money out but your partner can't get money behind your back.

A credit card will probably revert to the main name on the account. The additional name has to fill out a new application form and you won't automatically get one. Please avoid any temptation to go on a spending spree with a joint credit card just to teach your ex-spouse a lesson. You still have to repay any debts you run up. If you ignore them, you won't get a credit card in future.

You should also let the DSS know immediately you split up. Don't wait until you get divorced. You might be entitled to more benefits when you are on your own, particularly if you've got children. Whoever is responsible for bringing up the children might be able to get One Parent Benefit which is tax-free. You can claim this whether you are the father, mother, divorced,separated or unmarried. And the sooner you claim the better. Any older women who still pay the reduced rate married women's National Insurance stamp should start paying the full stamp otherwise they will lose pension.

PENSION

Pensions are a big problem. In the past, nearly every woman who got divorced lost out from her husband's pension. You should make sure you don't. You might have to go to court to sort it out.

The only pension you won't lose is the basic state pension. Even after you have divorced you can still claim on your husband's National Insurance contributions. But you won't get any of his State Earnings Related Pension Scheme (Serps). Neither will you get his company pension, however long you've been married. You lose your share of his pension money when he retires and you also lose a widow's pension if he dies before you. The company can't split the pension in half so he will have to give you money now to make up for it.He probably hasn't got any spare money. In that case, you should try to get a greater share of the house if you own it. Or a greater share of your joint valuables.

THE HOUSE

The biggest item to fight over is your home if you own it. One of you might want to stay put, in which case you'll have to buy the other one out. This involves getting a professional valuation and seeing the building society about a bigger mortgage. Even if your name is not on the deeds, you can't be thrown out while you are married. But the court will decide how long you can stay or whether the house has to be sold when you divorce.

Before you do anything else, you should register your right to the property. Contact the Land Registry in London or the building society for advice. That stops your spouse from selling the house without you knowing about it. Often, a husband pays the mortgage and a wife pays for everything else - the shopping, children's clothes, holidays and decorating equipment. When they split up he says the house is his because he has paid for it. She has nothing to show for all the money she has paid out over the years. The courts take this into account. If you take over the mortgage repayments, you must tell the bank or building society. And remember to claim the tax relief. If you are having difficulties keeping up the repayments, do let them know immediately and they will help you find a way to stay in your home. They are far more likely to stretch the rules a bit if you have kept them informed all down the line. Remember to pay the household insurance premiums as well. The last thing you need is a burglary or a fire and then find the insurance has run out.

If you are renting, the court can decide who carries on living in the property. The judge can transfer the tenancy from one partner to the other.

SOLICITORS

You might decide that you need a solicitor to help sort out the tangle. Perhaps your partner is not producing the financial information you need, or you receive a divorce petition and don't know what to do next. You might have used a solicitor in the past when you bought a house, but that doesn't mean they know anything about divorce. The best solicitor is one that a friend recommends. Otherwise, you can contact the Law Society and ask for a list of solicitors in your area who specialise in matrimonial law. You might be entitled to civil legal aid if you have very little money and your divorce is going to end up in court. You can claim whether you are defending a case or bringing it. You might have to pay some money back if you end up with a good settlement. Or you might be entitled to two hours of free advice under the Green Form scheme if it's an undefended divorce. A few solicitors run a £5 for half-an-hour scheme which anyone can use, regardless of how much money you earn.

YOUR WILL

Lastly, you should make out a new will. Your old will is not invalidated by divorce, but your ex-spouse is assumed to have died the day before the divorce. All your money goes to the other people named in your will. If there isn't anyone, your money is divided by law as though you had not made a will.

CHAPTER 12

WOMEN AND MONEY

EQUALITY between the sexes has come a long way since 1970 when women got the right to equal pay. Nearly 70% of women now work either full or part time. In many households, a woman's earnings are a vital part of the family budget.

In the past, women tended to leave the financial decisions to men. Today they are realising how important it is to be involved in planning their own financial futures. This is just as well because women's financial needs are often different to men's mainly because women's lives tend to follow a different pattern.

HOW WOMEN'S FINANCIAL NEEDS CHANGE

Single Women. Without family commitments, single women normally have most spending power. This is the time to save and put money aside for your pension to give you security and financial independence. But make sure these arrangements are flexible in case your circumstances change. A long term savings plan, such as an endowment, will not give good returns if you cash in early. National Savings products, TESSAs and Personal Equity Plans give you more flexibility.

Many single women are now buying their own homes. If

you don't have children or dependents, you don't need life cover so choose a repayment mortgage. But as you haven't a partner to help with the payments if you fall ill, you should take out an income replacement policy or critical illness cover.

Living Together. Many couples nowadays decide to live together instead of getting married. Women must be very careful in this situation because they don't have as many legal rights as they do within a marriage. You can find yourself at a financial disadvantage if you separate or your partner dies.

If you move into a property in your partner's name, you may not be entitled to a share in it even though you may be contributing to the household budget. If your partner dies without a will, his relatives will normally inherit his property. So make sure the property is in joint names. If you are unmarried, you will not be entitled to a widow's pension from your partner's pension scheme. So you will need to be sure you are making sufficient pension provision yourself.

Having children. Most women still give up work for some years to look after their family while their children are young. When they resume work, they often take a part time job - at least initially. This reduces their earning power severely and can have a devastating effect on their pension prospects which is why it is so important for women to put money into their pension when they have got money.

If you have a young family, it is particularly important to make sure that your partner has enough life insurance to protect you and your children against hardship in the event of his death. Make sure that any large debts, such as a mortgage, are covered. There should also be a lump sum that you can invest to make up for your partner's missing income. As a rough rule of thumb you should aim for an amount of around 10 times your partner's current yearly income. The cheapest types of life insurance are term insurance and unit linked whole life insurance.

To make sure you get the money promptly on your partner's death, make sure the money is put in trust for you and the children. The insurance company will provide a form to do this free of charge. This way the money won't be liable to Inheritance Tax and if your partner dies owing money, his creditors won't be able to get at it either.

More and more couples are also insuring women's lives so that a man does not suffer financial problems if his wife or partner dies, particularly if he has a family to look after. If you want to do this it is best to take out two separate policies. Joint life insurance policies are slightly cheaper but if you separate, these policies are often cancelled and you can lose money.

If you are married you can insure your husband's life, but if you are not it is best for your partner to take out insurance on his own life and name you as the beneficiary.

Divorce. Many marriages nowadays end in divorce and women often suffer financially as a result. You may get a share of the family home but you will probably have less to live on. If you have children and depend on your ex-husband's maintenance payments, remember to keep his life insured.

In the past, many women missed out because they did not claim a share of their husband's pension. If you have spent time off work bringing up children and have not contributed to your own pension scheme for very long, you face the prospect of having little more than the basic state pension to live on at retirement. So make sure your husband's pension - which is often his largest investment - is included in the reckoning, if you divorce.

Widowhood. Most women outlive their husbands or partners, so they face the prospect of coping alone financially at some time. This is why it is best to be involved in the financial decision making while your partner is alive. Make sure he makes a will. If you are left with money to invest when he dies, seek professional advice.

Your bank or building society can help. The best tips are to keep most of your money in low risk investments, such as National Savings products and building society accounts. And don't put all your eggs in one investment basket.

INDEPENDENT TAXATION FOR WOMEN

If you want to make the most of your money, whatever

your age or marital status, it is important to consider your tax position. Since April 1990, all women have been taxed independently, whether they are married or single. This means every woman now has her own personal tax allowance and is also responsible for completing her own tax returns, though fortunately you will not often be asked to do this unless you are self employed.

Previously, husbands were responsible for their wives' tax affairs so women had to tell their husbands about any savings. Under the present system you can have your own savings account and your husband doesn't need to know about it.

Your tax allowance is the amount of income you can receive from a job or from your savings without paying tax. Married couples receive an extra tax allowance which normally goes to the husband. But if your husband isn't working or has a low income and can't use up this allowance, it can be transferred to you to set against your income so that you can save tax. If you are a single parent you can also claim a larger allowance. Older women aged over 65 and 75 automatically get a higher tax allowance.

It is very important to make full use of your tax allowance. If you are working it may already be covered by your income. But if not, your tax allowance can still be put to good use because it can be set against income from savings. This means you can get the interest on your building society account, for example, free of tax. You just have to ask the building society for a form so that you can register as a non-taxpayer. Even if you have a joint account, the society may even be prepared to pay half of the interest without tax deducted. On other savings, where tax is already deducted, you can get a refund from the taxman. (Inland Revenue leaflet IR110, A Guide for People with Savings, gives details about how to claim tax refunds.)

Many married couples are still not taking advantage of the opportunity to save tax under independent taxation. This is possible if a husband is paying tax on his income and savings, and a wife is not. By transferring some savings to his wife or into a joint account, he will pay less tax and she will not have to pay tax either because her personal allowance can be used.

This can become particularly relevant after retirement. While most men receive a full state pension and often a company pension on top, this is rarely the case with women so their tax allowance is not used either. A transfer of savings from husband to wife will therefore both help to save tax and give her some income to make up for her missing pension.

Married couples also benefit because married women now have their own annual capital gains tax allowance. Previously, married couples shared one allowance. This makes it worthwhile to divide the ownership of investments such as shares and property if you have large capital gains.

If you are already paying tax on your income, you can cut the tax on your savings by putting them into tax efficient schemes such as TESSAs, National Savings Certificates, Tax Exempt Friendly Society Plans and Personal Equity Plans. Contributions to a pension plan are also a very tax efficient form of saving.

WOMEN AND PENSIONS

Women still give far too little thought to pensions. Yet bearing in mind that women on average live to over 80, it means you are ignoring around 20 years or more of your life if you don't plan for your retirement. Assuming your husband or the state will provide is a high risk strategy. Your marriage could break down and state pensions are steadily going down in value. The basic old age pension is currently worth only 17% of average earnings.

However, it is not always easy for women to make sufficient pension provision because of the breaks that often occur in their working lives when they bring up children and their lower earnings if they spend a period working part time. When you are considering your pension plans, this is something you need to consider. This is why it makes sense to put as much as you can into a pension plan while you are young and single. If you do take a break, when you return to work you should aim to try and make up for some of the lost time. It is almost impossible to contribute too much to a pension.

State pensions:

Many women currently reaching retirement do not qualify for a state pension in their own right because they opted to pay reduced National Insurance contributions. Their pension is based on their husband's contribution. But since 1977, this option has no longer been available.

Now women normally pay National Insurance contributions towards a basic state pension for themselves. If you stop work to look after children or elderly relatives, you receive credits. To qualify for a full basic state pension you must have paid or been credited with NI contributions for at least 39 years and this may increase in the future.

On top of the basic state pension you may also contribute towards the State Earnings Related Pension Scheme (SERPS) which will give you an extra pension related to your average level of earnings. Here women are disadvantaged because if you stop working for a few years, it brings down your average.

Nowadays it is possible to opt out of SERPS and have your contributions channelled into a private pension scheme instead. For younger women, there is a good prospect of a better pension if you opt out of SERPS initially. Before 1992, it was considered worthwhile for women up to around age 40. Now that the Government is giving fewer financial incentives, the cut off age has gone down to around 35. But for women who earn less than around £9,500 per year, opting out is not recommended whatever their age.

So if your earnings are insufficient or you are over the recommended age, it is better to go back into SERPS. But unfortunately, neither SERPS nor a replacement personal pension policy funded by SERPS contributions alone is likely to provide you with enough pension to live out your retirement in comfort. You will still need to make extra savings. The younger you are when you make these contributions the better because they will have longer to grow.

Company Pensions:

The ideal solution is to join a good company pension

scheme. The advantage is that your employer will also make contributions to the scheme on your behalf. An increasing number of pension schemes today accept part-timers as well as full timers.

One of the snags is that if you leave your job within two years of becoming a member of a company pension scheme, your contributions alone will be refunded. If this happens you must resist the temptation to spend this money at all costs. You will regret it in the long run. Put it into a personal pension policy instead or, if you are stopping work, invest it in something like a Personal Equity Plan where it can build up free of tax until your retirement.

If you join an employer's scheme after a break bringing up a family, you could make up for some lost time by putting in additional savings. These are known as additional voluntary contributions (AVCs).

Personal Pensions:

If your employer does not have a pension scheme, you can take out a personal pension policy. If you already have a policy because you have opted out of SERPS, bear in mind that the final pension will still be quite small so it is a good idea to make further savings of your own.

A personal pension may also be a good idea even if your employer does have a pension scheme, if you know you will definitely be leaving within two years.

To get the best out of a monthly premium personal pension plan you need to save regularly until your retirement. You will lose out heavily if you start a plan and then stop saving within two or three years because a high proportion of your initial premiums are absorbed in costs. So make sure you pitch your premiums at an affordable level and if you think you may have to stop saving for a while, check whether the insurance company will let you stop and restart your premiums without penalty.

An even better strategy if you don't think you can keep up regular premiums - but it needs a lot more self discipline - is to save in an ordinary savings account until you have built up a lump sum of say £500. You can then invest in what is known as a single premium personal pension policy. You will still get tax relief. The advantage is that the charges on these policies are low and you are not penalised if you cannot keep up your savings.

Your Pension When You Are Not Working:

One of the problems of pension plans is that you can only contribute to them when you are working. If you take a career break to bring up children or care for elderly relatives you must stop contributing. But this should not stop you from saving towards your retirement if you are able to. Your partner may be willing to help by transferring money into your name in order to benefit from independent taxation as explained above. When you return to work you may be able to invest the savings you have built up in a single premium personal pension plan and then claim tax relief.

AT RETIREMENT

Under your own pension scheme, you can often decide whether you want to take part of your pension as a lump sum. This is usually a good idea as it gives you more flexibility. If you have a personal pension plan, remember to make use of your freedom to shop around for the best pension at retirement. Ask a professional adviser for help.

If you are married, it is very important to find out about your husband's company or personal pension and what benefit you will get if he dies before you. Under a personal pension policy and under some company schemes, he will have a choice at retirement as to whether a pension is paid to you after his death or not, and at what level - often it is a half of what he gets while he is alive. He may also be able to decide whether he gets a fixed pension, or one which increases in value each year. Make sure he takes your interests into account and chooses a pension that continues after his death because it is highly likely that you will outlive him.

CHAPTER 13

PENSIONS

There are more than ten million retired people in Britain today. They include a small but growing minority who have never had it so good - able to afford most of the good things in life, including one or even two holidays abroad each year.

But for the vast majority retirement is at best a time to eke out a private pension, which may be eroded by inflation, or at worst having a State pension which is not sufficient to live on.

It is estimated that about HALF of all pensioner households depend upon at least some help from the State. One thing is certain. With the recent advances in medicine most of us will survive to a ripe old age.

According to Keith Hughes, one of Britain's leading retirement counsellors, retirement should be the longest holiday of your lifetime.

Keith tells me it means you have an extra 3,000 hours leisure time to fill each year.

But if you haven't the money to enjoy it retirement can seem more like a long prison sentence than a well earned break.

Most people nowadays can choose what it is to be by deciding whether they're prepared to tuck away enough now to provide a decent pension in future.

The younger you are the less conscious you are of the need for a pension. Yet the younger you start the less of a burden it is. If you began putting 5 per cent of your earnings into a pension plan at thirty you could expect a pension worth a third of your earnings by 65. Wait until 45 before starting and it would be little more than a tenth.

THE OLD AGE PENSION

Until quite recently all that people could count on for their old age was the basic State pension - now £56.10 for a single person and £89.80 for a couple.

Most people qualify for at least that so long as they've been paying their National Insurance contributions regularly.

Many people who paid "graduated contributions" between 1961 and 1975 may get a small supplement on top.

The State pension increases year by year in line with the cost of living. But that's all. Past Governments also gave increases to keep it in line with rises in average earnings but that was stopped by the present Government to save taxpayers' money. It's just about enough to live on but it won't stretch to foreign holidays.

THE STATE EARNINGS RELATED PENSION SCHEME (SERPS)

In the late 1970s following an agreement between the main political parties the Government introduced the State Earnings Related Pension Scheme aimed at giving a decent pension to all company employees by the end of the century.

Everybody at work was expected to chip in more now in order to get more later on.

The plan was to give you an extra pension equal to about a quarter of average pay on top of the State pension - currently about one fifth of average wages for a single person and a third for a retired couple.

That would have meant retiring on a pension getting on for half of what you were earning.

But in the middle 1980s the Thatcher Government decided it could no longer afford this and started chopping back SERPS severely. The pension it provides will be steadily scaled down from the turn of the century so that people retiring in 2010 will get an overall State pension of less than a quarter of average earnings - about the same as people were getting in 1978 before SERPs began. So you can no longer

144

depend upon the State system to keep you comfortably in your old age.

COMPANY SCHEMES

Most people now enjoying a comfortable retirement were in a company pension scheme.

Eleven million working people Britain are covered by such schemes which should provide them with a decent regular income when they retire ON TOP of the State old age pension.

The best of these offer a pension of up to two thirds of what you were earning just before you clocked in for the last time.

They're called "sixtieths " schemes because they provide a pension equal to a sixtieth of pay for each year you're in the plan. So forty years in the company scheme should qualify for forty sixtieths or two thirds of your final pay packet.

If you're lucky this pension will be fully price protected. But only annual increases of 3 or 5 per cent are likely to be guaranteed.

You normally have the right to take part of your pension as a tax free cash lump sum when you retire.

Other benefits normally include a decent widow's pension payable should you die before or after you retire and some life insurance cover.

Employees' contributions to such schemes are normally 5p out of every Pound you earn.

Your boss pays the rest which is often twice what you pay.

These schemes are the best for most workers.

But there are drawbacks. If you leave some time before retirement age, for example, you lose out badly.

For the pension you'll then receive is linked to what you were earning when you left the company - not to what you will be earning elsewhere when you eventually retire.

You'll get some increases to allow for the rise in the cost of living since you left until you retire. But this is restricted to a maximum of five per cent a year - no matter how high the rate of inflation rises.

You may get a better deal when you change jobs by

arranging to take with you the pension rights you have clocked up so far. These could be added into the scheme at your next employer. Or you could put them into a pension plan of your own with an insurance company or pensions firm.

You may do better than leaving your pension rights behind. But you still come off worse than had you stayed put.

(Normally public sector employees are much better treated, especially if they change jobs within the sector.)

One way to avoid this problem altogether is to take out a personal pension plan instead of joining the firm's pension scheme. If you're still young and likely to change jobs frequently this might be a good idea. You could then join the pension scheme of the firm you eventually settle down with later on in life.

But you must have the discipline to start your plan and keep it going.

ADDITIONAL VOLUNTARY CONTRIBUTIONS

Many people in company pension schemes don't get the biggest possible pensions.

The scheme may only count your basic pay, leaving out bonuses and overtime.

You may not join until your reach your thirties or forties with not much pension to show from previous jobs.

And if you're a mum, you may have taken a five or ten year break from paid work.

But you can boost your pension rights with Additional Voluntary Contributions (AVCs for short). Your extra monthly payments get full tax relief at your top tax rate and when you retire the money you have invested provides you with extra pension.

They can be made either through your firm or invested elsewhere when they're called Free Standing Additional Voluntary contributions - FSAVCs for short.

To find out more ask your pensions manager at work or talk to a pensions adviser.

PERSONAL PENSIONS

More than half of all workers either work for themselves or for firms which don't offer a decent company pension scheme.

Their best answer is to start their own PERSONAL PENSION plan. You could get yourself just as good a pension on your own- if you're prepared to pay for it. As a bare minimum you should chip at least 5p out of every £ you earn and step up your contributions regularly as your income improves.

But to match a company scheme, where the employer would be contributing as much as you, you'd have put in nearer 10 per cent of what you earn.

Men under 40 and women under 35 working for a company and earning at least £9,500 a year should also consider opting out of the State Earnings Related Pension Scheme (SERPS).

Part of your own and your employer's National Insurance gets added instead to your personal pension plan.

For younger people it should clock up more pension rights for you than it would in SERPs.

Take a man aged 35 earning £15,000 a year. If he stays in SERPs his contributions for this year will earn him £55 extra yearly state pension at 65.

In a decent personal pension those same contributions should produce considerably more - anything from £64 to as much as £131 depending upon on how well your plan does.

For a woman aged 30 a similar plan should produce anything between £54 and £114 yearly pension at 60 from this year's contributions.

But remember you can't opt out of SERPS unless all the money saved is going into either a personal pension plan or a company scheme.

Leading insurance firms will let you start plans with your former SERPs contributions only.

But to achieve a really worthwhile pension at retirement it is simply not enough just to switch your contributions out of the State scheme.

Sadly of the five million who have already opted out of SERPS already no fewer than two million haven't bothered to do anything more. And many of the rest are putting in only token amounts.

Yet contributing to a pension plan, private or occupational, is one of the best investments you could possibly make:

● Your contributions are tax deductible at your top tax rate. So for a basic rate taxpayer every £1 you put in costs you only 75p while the cost for a higher rate payer falls to 60p.

● Your money is invested in what is called a "gross" fund which means that any interest, dividends or profits your contributions earn are pretty much tax free.

● You can choose when you wish to retire and start collecting your pension from age fifty in a personal pension and from the age agreed by your firm in a company scheme. But that part of the fund built up with the National Insurance contributions added into it can't be turned into pension until you reach 65 if you're a man and 60 if you're a woman.

And you are entitled to take part of it as a tax free lump sum. The very least you should put in is 5 per cent of what you're now earning.

And you should increase your contributions year by year in line with any rises in your income.

Take a man aged 35 on £15,000 as year. If he chipped in 5 per cent - £750 a year or £62.50 a month - it would cost him less than £47 a month after basic rate tax relief.

If his fund grew at eight and a half per cent a year he could expect to collect a tax free lump sum of £19,800 at 65 plus a pension for life of £6,860 a year - about £572 a month or £132 a week.

If the fund did better still and grew at, say, 13 per cent, he might instead get £45,700 tax free plus £17,700 yearly pension - £1,465 per month or £340 a week.

These figures are a rough guide. They assume that you make level contributions and no inflation. In the real world, of course, your contributions should increase in line with earnings, which on past form should keep you ahead of rising prices.

WHERE TO INVEST IT

There are plenty of investment firms to choose from to run your PERSONAL PENSION PLAN.

Only time will tell which will produce the best pension. But past investment performance is some guide.

Leading life insurance firms have been longest in the pensions business as well.

Among the most consistent performers are in alphabetical order, Commercial Union, Equitable Life, Friends Provident, General Accident, Legal & General, Prudential, Scottish Amicable, Scottish Life, Scottish Widows, Standard Life, and Sun Life.

By all means get quotes from firms such as these. But it also makes sense to seek independent advice. For the name of your nearest independent adviser ring 0483 461 461.

TAKING STOCK

Review your pensions position regularly. That advice comes from one of the top brains in the industry - Legal and General's pensions controller, Ron Spill.

And that includes women who often have to depend heavily on their partner's pension.

The DSS can give you a forecast of your State pension.

Your Company should be giving you a regular benefit statement and your life insurance or investment company can do the same with your own personal pension plan.

Tot them up and if they leave you short of the pension you'd like to retire on, take expert advice on what to do.

FRAUD

How safe is your pension?

Thieving tycoon Robert Maxwell made off with £450 million belonging to people who worked for his companies. Since then many more pensions frauds have come to light.

The Government is now planning to tighten up the rules

governing pensions. Meanwhile what can YOU do to ensure YOUR pension is secure?

If you belong to a COMPANY pension scheme your money is as safe as the people to whom you have entrusted it.

Ideally you and your fellow workers should have your own representatives on the trustees keeping an eye on it for you.

That's especially important if the fund is being run "in house" rather than being managed by reputable outside investment experts.

But in either case the actual funds - the money and securities - ought to be held by an outside trustee such as a major bank, which is above reproach.

No matter how it is run here are some tips to ensure your money is safe:

ASK for a regular copy of the trustees' annual report. A good scheme should send it to you automatically.

The report will tell you who the auditors and bankers are and where your money is invested.

The scheme should NOT share the same auditors and bankers as the company.

TRY to get your own representatives on to the trustees.

CHECK that not more than 5 per cent of the pension fund is invested in your boss's business or any related businesses.

And watch out if the pension scheme suddenly buys the factory or the company's headquarters building!

WORRY if you hear about any delays in people getting their pensions or transfers to other schemes by colleagues leaving the company.

If you have A PERSONAL PENSION PLAN make sure you pick a tip top investment firm whose reputation is above reproach.

And make sure that all cheques and payments are made out direct to the firm and not to any salesmen or other investment adviser.

You are a little better protected than people in company schemes. For if the investment firm you pick goes bust or the managers run off with your money there is an Investors

Compensation Scheme which would cover you for up to £48,000 of any loss.

CHAPTER 14

PLANNING FOR RETIREMENT

A PENSION should be the cornerstone of your retirement plans - but it should not be the only link in the chain. As you get nearer to the start of the longest holiday of your life, you should be paying the maximum you are allowed into your pension fund. Any surplus cash should be tucked away in other forms of investments so that you build up a nice little nest egg when the gold watch time arrives.

INVESTING ON RETIREMENT

Your pension, plus whatever you have managed to save, generally has to last you for the rest of your life. This is a sobering thought and has the effect of concentrating the mind on maximising the most from your investments. The same principles apply as when you were saving up for your retirement. You have to strike the right balance between the risks you are prepared to take and whether your main objective is to go for capital growth or increase your income levels. If you have a good pension and perhaps a part time job, you may not need the income and you can go for growth. If your pension is on the low side, you will need to make your investments work harder to produce more interest to top up your spending power.

But for most retired people the most important factor is

safety - you cannot afford to lose any of your hard earned capital. This is why safety first investments are generally the order of the day.

You will still need your savings account which gives you quick access to your cash. If you are still a taxpayer, keep up your TESSAs.

SAFETY FIRST
National Savings Accounts

The Government offers a variety of accounts which are totally safe although often unexciting.

● Income Bonds. You invest a lump sum, minimum £2,000, maximum £250,000. Income is paid monthly without tax deducted although you will eventually have to pay it if you are a taxpayer. If you cash the bond within the first 12 months of buying it, the interest is reduced by half.

● Capital Bonds. Similar to National Savings Certificates in that you have to invest for five years to get the best return. The longer you hold the bond, the higher the rate of interest. You can invest between £100 and £250,000. Interest is taxable and although it is not paid to you until the end of the five year period, taxpayers will still have to pay tax on the anticipated amount every year.

● FIRST option bond. The First stands for Fixed Interest Rate Savings tax paid. It is a one year bond with the interest rate guaranteed for that period. Basic rate tax is deducted from the interest and you will be penalised if you do not hold the bond for the full year. You can invest between £1,000 and £250,000.

● Index-linked Savings Certificates - popularly known as Granny Bonds. Well worth having as they protect your capital against inflation. And offer a tax free bonus if held for five years.

● Gilts - short for gilt-edged securities - are in effect loans to the Government. They pay a guaranteed rate of interest but they are also traded on the stock exchange in much the same way as shares. Their capital value can change in line with changes in interest rates but when they are due to be repaid by the Government, - the redemption date - you are guaranteed to get the capital sum back. You have to pay tax on the interest but you can also make capital gains which will be free of tax. It is cheaper to buy gilts from the National Savings Register rather than a stockbroker who will charge a higher rate of commission. You can also buy gilts via a managed gilt fund run by a bank or an insurance company. This works in much the same way as a unit trust where investors' cash is pooled together to give a bigger spread of investments.

● Guaranteed Income Bonds. These are bonds issued by insurance companies which guarantee you a fixed rate over an agreed period - generally between one and five years. They are not recommended for non-taxpayers as basic rate tax is deducted from the interest and cannot be reclaimed.

TAKING A RISK

Taking a risk with your savings normally means linking your money to some form of stock market investment. If this is going to cause you sleepless nights, don't do it. But you should remember that if you belonged to a company pension scheme, or had a personal pension, the fund managers probably put your cash in a wide spread of investments, including shares. Most financial experts agree that to protect the future value of your money, as well as increase your capital, you should have some stockmarket-based investments.

This does not mean that you have to do the investing yourself. If your financial position allows it, you can still invest in unit trusts or investment trusts and use the expertise of professional fund managers. And Peps can still play a useful role after you retire simply because of their big tax advantages. Other low risk investments you may consider are:

* Permanent Interest Bearing Shares. (PIBS). These are shares issued by several of the major building societies. They can be bought and sold on the stock exchange and they pay a fixed rate of interest. Their capital value goes up and down in line with the movements in interest rates and it is possible to lose money on them as well as make capital profits. Do not confuse them with ordinary building society accounts which are protected if a society collapses. In the unlikely event of a society going to the wall, Pibs would be

the last in line to be paid off. Because there is this slight element of risk, the interest you get is generally higher than national savings or other building society accounts. Interest is paid after deducting standard rate tax which can be reclaimed by non-taxpayers. No capital gains tax is paid on profits.

● Cash Unit Trusts. Instead of investing in shares, some unit trusts invest in cash deposits. Because they deal in such large amounts of money, the rates they get are generally better than you can get from a bank or building society, though you have to pay management charges. Some trusts allow instant withdrawals and even give you a cheque book.

● Utilities Funds. A recent addition to the unit trust range. Your money is placed in the companies which run our every day basics such as gas and electricity. Although the value of the units can go down as well as up, they are generally regarded as being stable investments which are less risky than most and offer the chance of a good income and modest capital growth.

● Preference shares. These are shares issued by big companies which carry a fixed annual dividend. You have to buy them through a stockbroker but returns are good and if you choose household names, the risk is low.

AGE ALLOWANCE

One of the perks of getting older is increased tax allowances. These extra age allowances are given to help older people manage on what is probably a reduced income. However, if you are rich enough not to need this extra help, the taxman takes it back. "Rich enough" means an income of more than £14,200 for the tax year 1993/4. You lose £1 in tax allowance for every £2 of income above the limit. This works out at a very high rate of tax so if your income is around the £14,200 mark, it is worthwhile doing a little homework to avoid paying the extra tax by reducing your income below the magic figure.

This means investing in tax free areas such as National Savings certificates or Tessas. You may also consider with-profit bonds where you can generally take a small amount of tax free income every year. The other way of avoiding income tax is to aim for capital gains by investing in safe areas such as Government Securities popularly known as "gilts". All capital gains on gilts are tax free and for other gains you currently have a tax free allowance of £5,800 each year.

RAISING EXTRA CASH

The phrase "house rich, cash poor" is often used to describe older people who have a valuable asset in their property - but not enough cash to run it or enjoy a comfortable life style. The mortgage has probably been repaid years ago and although house prices may have fallen in the nineties the property may still be worth a tidy sum. There are two basic ways of making your house work for you and raising some extra money. The first is generally called a home income plan or mortgage annuity and the second is a home reversion scheme.

Home Income Plan

This type of plan involves taking out a mortgage on the property and using the cash to buy an annuity. The income from the annuity goes to pay the mortgage interest and what is left over is yours to spend. How much you get depends on your age, sex and interest rates at the time but as with all annuities, the older you are the more you receive. A home income plan is not generally worthwhile unless you are aged at least 70 - a combined age of 150 if you are a couple - and the property has to be freehold or on a long lease. Other points to note are:

● Often the maximum loan is limited to £30,000 which is the limit for tax relief on the interest.

● You can usually take up to 10 per cent of the loan in cash which is useful if you need some urgent spending money.

● The loan is interest only and the rate can be fixed at the start or vary with rate changes. Most older people prefer a fixed rate so they know exactly where they stand.

● The loan is repaid from the sale of the property when you or your surviving partner dies.

● Many plans have a "capital protection" clause which says that if you die within the first few years, only part of the loan has to be repaid.

● Make sure that the extra income you get does not put you in a higher tax bracket. You should also make sure that the extra cash will not affect any social security benefits which you may be receiving.

Home Reversion Scheme

Instead of raising a mortgage on your house, a reversion scheme allows you to sell all or part of it to the company who hands over the cash. You and your spouse can live in the property for the rest of your life but when the surviving partner dies, the house goes to the reversion company. You can normally raise more cash than a home income plan but the big disadvantage is that you will not be able to leave the property to your family. In addition, the value put on the house by the reversion company will generally be much lower than what it is actually worth. Some reversion schemes allow you to sell a percentage of your home, say half, then a few years later you can raise more money by selling the balance.

There has been some bad publicity about some types of home income plans. These are normally based on invest-ment bonds - and the cash raised by selling your home is placed in a bond. The major drawback is that if the bond declines in value your income payments will fall, causing major headaches. Always make sure your home income plan is a member of SHIP - which stands for Safe Home Income Plans, and is backed by Charity Age Concern. More details from the Secretary, Cecil Hinton, on 081 390 8160.

WILLS AND INHERITANCE TAX

Although wills are often discussed towards the end of a chapter, in real life you should make a will long before you reach the end of your days. Only one in three people bother, probably on the assumption that they do not have very much to leave. But if you own a property, no matter how small, you own an estate and it is only fair to your family to leave instructions as to its disposal. One other good reason why you should make a will when you are younger concerns young children. If both parents were to die in an accident, a will can specify who they want to become guardians and responsible for their future upbringing.

● Intestacy. If you do not make a will, the state divides up your money for you. There are set rules laid down to do this. If you live together but are not married, surviving partners could find themselves with nothing. Common law wives and husbands generally have no rights unless a will specifies who gets what.

HOW TO WRITE A WILL

The safest way is to go to a solicitor. Simple wills will probably cost no more than £50 although if your estate is more complicated, the price will rise. In any case, a complex estate means legal advice to avoid paying too much tax (see below). You can also go to a will writing agency where the fees can be around £30 and the wording is generally checked by a solicitor. There is nothing to stop you buying a will form from a stationers and writing it your yourself. Do follow the instructions carefully as mistakes can invalidate the will.

Revoking a will

The will stands until you make another one. You can also add bits to it - called codicils. Marriage generally revokes a will in its entirety but divorce does not. If your domestic circumstances change, it is vitally important to update or rewrite a will.

INHERITANCE TAX

One of the main reasons you write a will is to specify who gets what. At the same time it is the most important way of avoiding inheritance tax which is what the taxman takes from your assets before your family can take the balance. At present no inheritance tax is payable if your estate is worth less than £150,000. The excess is taxed at 40%.

How to avoid it

● The seven year rule. You can make gifts before you die

and provided you live for seven years after the gift has been made, no inheritance tax is payable. If you die within the seven years the tax is paid on a reduced sliding scale. It has to be a genuine gift to qualify and you are not allowed to keep control over the item.

● Husband and Wife. Gifts between husband and wife are free of tax.

● Small gifts. You can each give away £3,000 a year and this amount can also be carried back for one tax year if it has not been used up. In addition you can make small gifts up to £250 to as many different people as you like.

● Wedding presents. A parent can give up to £5,000 to the happy couple free of inheritance tax. A grandparent can give £2,500 and anyone else £1,000.

INSURANCE

If you think your estate is going to be clobbered by tax, look at some form of life insurance. Specialist advice will be needed but it is possible to take out a term insurance policy which will be paid to your beneficiaries when you die so that the tax can be covered.